P9-DLZ-491

Magic Stack-n-Whack QUILTS

Bethany S. Reynolds

American Quilter's Society
P. O. Box 3290 • Paducah, KY 42002-3290

Located in Paducah, Kentucky, the American Quilter's Society (AQS) is dedicated to promoting the accomplishments of today's quilters. Through its publications and events, AQS strives to honor today's quiltmakers and their work and inspire future creativity and innovation in quiltmaking.

EDITOR: TERRI NYMAN
TECHNICAL EDITOR: BONNIE K. BROWNING
BOOK DESIGN: ANGELA SCHADE
ILLUSTRATIONS: BETHANY S. REYNOLDS
COVER DESIGN: TERRY WILLIAMS AND ANGELA SCHADE
PHOTOGRAPHY: CHARLES R. LYNCH

Library of Congress Cataloging-in-Publication Data

Reynolds, Bethany
     Magic stack-n-whack quilts / Bethany Reynolds
              p.   cm.
    ISBN 1-57432-704-6
    1. Patchwork--Patterns.   2. Quilting--Patterns.   3. Kaleidoscopes in art.
                      I. Title.
TT835.R459   1997
746.46'041--dc21   97-46322
                                         CIP

Additional copies of this book may be ordered from American Quilter's Society, PO Box 3290, Paducah, KY 42002-3290 @ $19.95.

Copyright© 1998, Bethany S. Reynolds

17th Printing

This book or any part thereof may not be reproduced without the written consent of the author and publisher. Exception: the author and publisher give permission to photocopy pages 98, 103–109 for personal use only. The information and patterns in this book have been provided in good faith. The American Quilter's Society has no control of materials or methods used and, therefore, is not responsible for the use of or results obtained from this information.

Contents

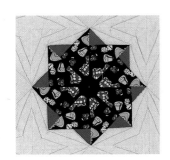

Acknowledgments

Thanks go first and always to my husband, Bill, my longtime partner in the best sense of the word; and to my son, Sam, for bringing me joy with his unique perspective. Thanks also to my parents, who are lifelong learners and teachers, for passing on the love of both pursuits.

I am indebted to Joanna Ellis for her generous and patient assistance with my computer queries. I am also grateful to several groups of quilters, including my workshop students, whose enthusiasm inspired me to write this book; my "quilt-lab rats," on-line and off, who bravely tested the "beta" versions of these projects; and especially my dear friends Kathleen Cravens, Ellie Carlisle, Pat Easa, Eleanor Guthrie, and Dottie Krueger, for their faith and friendship.

Thank you to Justin Hancock of Hancock Fabrics, Paducah, Kentucky, for permitting a photo shoot in the store and for letting me find the "magic" fabrics on their shelves.

Preface

In days of yore, wizards amazed and entertained kings and queens with their magic tricks. Through their mysterious, ancient arts, they conjured up marvelous surprises. Even today, sophisticated, modern audiences flock to magic shows to be dazzled. The wave of a wand and smoke and mirrors were all that were needed to conjure up flowers or a beautiful woman. This is an apt description for the designs in this book, for quilters can watch wonderfully intricate quilts appear with an ease that is nearly magical.

To create your own Magic Stack-n-Whack quilt, you will not need to use wands, mirrors or smoke, and you will not have to trace countless fabric patches with window templates. You just let a great fabric print do the work with the help of basic rotary-cutting equipment. Cutting the fabric for the blocks takes remarkably little time, and as you piece each unique and unexpected block, you experience the real magic. Like a fascinating magic act, the process will leave you spellbound and awed by the enchanting results.

Introduction

Kaleidoscope-effect quilts, in which a symmetrical design radiates from the center of the block, draw the admiration and envy of many quilters. Just as hand-held kaleidoscopes fascinate children of all ages, the intricacy, order, and mysterious changeability of these quilted creations attract us, but these quilt designs traditionally require much careful planning and cutting. Weeks can go by before the first seam gets sewn! While some quilters relish this part of the project, for others, it can be a tedious ordeal, an intimidating obstacle, or simply a "turn-off."

The designs in this book allow you to create exciting effects with fabric quickly and easily. The Stack-n-Whack method does not involve mirrors or window templates, and it works with a wide variety of fabrics, not just border stripes or symmetrical prints. The method used to create these designs involves layering and cutting fabric repeats with standard rotary cutting equipment. The resulting blocks are all unique. The exciting patterns happen spontaneously, without extensive planning or precision cutting. The experience is similar to making a mystery quilt. There is an element of faith and a certain risk involved that add to the fun, making the process as appealing as the finished product. Chapters One and Two contain information you will need to know for all the projects, including the stacking method that produces the kaleidoscope effects. Even if you are in a hurry to get started, please read these chapters before you begin whacking!

Chapters Three through Seven contain projects. Each chapter describes the Stack-n-Whack method for a particular shape, such as a 45° diamond, along with yardage requirements, piecing directions, and assembly instructions for designs based on that shape.

Chapter Eight contains suggestions for quilting and finishing your project.

Whether you are looking for a way to create a dazzling quilt in a few days or whether you are simply a quilter who loves to play with fabric, I am confident you will love making and showing off your Magic Stack-n-Whack quilts. I have been teaching these techniques for several years, watching quilters get caught up in the excitement, and hearing the exclamations of appreciation as each beautiful new block goes up on the wall. Many students tell me that their families are especially impressed with their creations; they don't realize how easy it is, and we don't need to tell them!

Chapter One
Backstage

Setting the Stage: Fabric Selection

The "magic" works best when you choose a print you love.

Selecting the fabric is the first step in making your quilt. We are lucky to have an abundance of luscious prints from which to choose, and many of them lend themselves beautifully to these designs.

The standard 100% cotton fabric sold for quilting is easy to work with, and if you have not had a lot of quilting experience, this is your best choice. Lightweight drapery chintz offers some tantalizing possibilities, too. Cotton blends will be harder to work with, as they tend to shift while you are cutting and sewing them.

Finding a suitable fabric should not be difficult. Settling on just one may be the hard part. A few simple guidelines will get you off to a great start.

The Main Fabric

The main fabric is the one that forms the kaleidoscope effect. This fabric sets the tone for the finished quilt.

Large florals and leaf prints are a natural choice for these quilts, but abstract prints and ethnic designs offer interesting alternatives (Plates 1A–F).

Have you ever spotted a striking large-scale print and thought, "That's wonderful, but what would I do with it?" The odds are it is a "magic" print. Novelty prints such as animals,

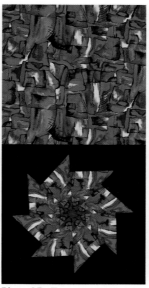

Plates 1A–B   Plate 1C   Plates 1D–E   Plate 1F

Plates 1A–F: (1A) Leaf print; (1B) JANUARY THAW, detail; (1C) examples of floral and leaf prints for main fabric; (1D) abstract print; (1E) STAINED GLASS, detail; and (1F) abstract and ethnic designs offer interesting possibilities.

fish, seasonal motifs, and scenics make exciting quilts for adults as well as children (Plates 2A–G). Do not overlook the markdown table at your favorite shop. Sometimes you will find unusual first-quality prints that are so unusual that no one seems to know how to use them. These "ugly ducklings" may be just waiting for you to unlock their true potential.

A bold, high-contrast print can result in a dramatic quilt, while a more subdued print may produce a softer, intricate effect (Plates 3A–D).

Look for a print that is medium to large in scale. You can get an idea of whether a print will be large enough by laying your hand flat on the fabric alongside the selvage (Plate 4).

Plates 2A–B   Plate 2C–D   Plates 2E–F   Plate 2G

Plates 3A–B   Plates 3C–D   Plate 4

Plates 2A–G, Plates 3A–D. Plate 4: (2A) Zoo print; (2B) SAM'S MENAGERIE, detail; (2C) Christmas novelty print; (2D) CHRIST-MAS MORNING STAR, detail; (2E) casino novelty print; (2F) STACKED DECK, detail; (2G) novelty prints and seasonal designs are fun to Stack-n-Whack; (3A) low contrast print used for CRYSTAL STAR; (3B) CRYSTAL STAR, detail; (3C) high contrast print used for CAROUSELS; (3D) CAROUSELS, detail; (4) the "hand test"—this print is too small-scale for most of the projects.

If your hand covers more than one of a particular motif, the print is probably too small in scale to be effective.

As you consider a fabric, disregard the colors for a moment and study the lines and shapes in the print. Are all the motifs similar in size and shape, or do they vary? A good variety will make for more interesting blocks (Plates 5A–B). Prints that combine geometric lines with more rounded shapes can be especially attractive (Plates 6A–B). Floral stripes and border prints can be effective as long as they fit the criteria for scale and variety. Sharp-edged designs, such as prints that have a thin black or gold outline around the motifs or a strongly contrasting background, help define the kaleidoscope effect. You can

Plate 5A Plate 5B Plate 6A–6B

Plates 7A–7B Plate 7C Plate 7D

Plates 5A–B, Plates 6A–B, Plates 7A–D: (5A) For the main print, avoid fabrics that have only a few shapes; (5B) greater variety of motifs in these prints creates more interesting blocks; (6A) combination of straight lines and curves in this botanical print adds punch to BOTANNICA; (6B) BOTANNICA, detail; (7A) the black background and gold outline give crisp definition to this tropical print; (7B) HOFFMAN CHALLENGE 1995, detail. Gold quilting enhances the distinctive motifs; (7C) the sharp edges of these prints produce more defined kaleidoscope effects; (7D) these soft-edged prints may be more "forgiving."

use prints that have softer outlines to help disguise less-than-perfect piecing (Plates 7A–D, page 9).

Look at the background around the motifs in your fabric. You need to keep in mind that you will be whacking random sections of the print rather than precision cutting the motifs. A print that has closely spaced motifs, or one in which the background has some texture (Plate 8A), will be a better choice than one that has large areas of plain background (Plate 8B), which might result in some empty-looking blocks.

Now, consider the colors in the print. The Stack-n-Whack cutting method tends to concentrate and intensify the colors in each of the blocks. For example, the print used for the quilt named 48 Parrot Diamond Ring (Plate 42, page 50) has parrots with plumage in various combinations of blue, green, yellow, red, and violet (Plate 9B). The block in Plate 9A isolates the cool blue and green tones, while the block in Plate 9C shows off the parrots' splashy red feathers. Generally, the more distinct the colors are in the print, the more variety you will have in the finished blocks.

Plate 8A

Plate 8B

Plates 9A–C

Plates 8A–B, Plates 9A–C: (8A) Look for prints with closely packed motifs or with some background texture; (8B) avoid prints with large areas of plain background; (9A) this block isolates the blue and green areas of the print; (9B) the multi-colored fabric used for 48 PARROT DIAMOND RING; (9C) another block features the red feathers.

It is a good idea to choose a print you love. This is the best way to ensure that you will love both the quiltmaking process and the finished quilt.

About Design Repeats

The amount of fabric needed for the kaleidoscope blocks will depend on the length of the design repeat in your chosen fabric, which can vary considerably (Plate 10). Fabric designers work within the technical confines of the manufacturing process. Most mills that are printing quilt fabrics use rotary screens, and these screens typically have a circumference of either 25¼" or 36". The measurement of the circumference is the vertical printing repeat of the fabric. On fabrics with a brand name on the selvage, you can easily spot the repeat size because the selvage information usually appears once each printed repeat.

Plate 10: These prints have design repeats ranging from 8" to 24". The horizontal lines indicate one design repeat on each fabric.

The fabric designer can choose to use the entire printing repeat length as a design repeat or divide the screen measurement into equal sections. This means that a fabric printed with a 36" screen, for example, could have a vertical design repeat of 36", 18", 12", 9", 6", or fewer inches.

The designer also decides on a horizontal (crosswise) repeat. For the projects in this book, you will not need to consider the repeat across the width. All fabric yardages are based on the vertical (lengthwise) design repeat length. In working with a great many fabrics, I have found that even high-quality prints are often slightly distorted across the width. This distortion may be imperceptible when the fabric is on the bolt, and for most quilting projects it would be of no consequence, but because kaleidoscope effects depend on symmetry, it is important to cut the pieces for each block from identical repeats. The lengthwise repeat is very consistent on most fabrics. Workshop students of mine who tried using repeats from across the width of the fabric found that the minor variations were magnified in the finished blocks. By using only lengthwise repeats, you will get the best results for your efforts.

Design Repeat and Yardage

When you have found a fabric you would like to use for the main fabric in your project, measure the print along one selvage from the beginning of one motif to the beginning of the next repeat of the same motif to determine the design repeat length. Check the yardage chart for your project to find the amount of fabric needed for that repeat length.

You will notice that shorter repeat lengths require less yardage. This does not mean that short repeat fabrics are the best choice, unless expense is your primary concern. As a rule, you will get more effective kaleidoscope blocks with longer design repeats (11" and longer). Prints with a repeat of 11" to 14" offer a good balance of scale and economy for most projects. Prints with 15" to 27" repeats can be even more effective, and you will not need a great deal of extra yardage for larger quilt projects. If you use a large repeat on a small project, you will have leftovers. I do not like to use the term "waste," because fabric is not wasted unless you throw it out. Use the extra for another project or get a friend started on Stack-n-Whack quilts and trade your leftovers.

If you have fallen in love with a fabric that has a short repeat (under 11"), consider choosing a project with smaller blocks. The batik fabric in Plate 11A has a 6" repeat and limited colors, making it a poor choice for the 10" block used in the Diamond Ring bed quilt. In the 6" block of the wall quilt, though, the subtle variations in the print have a chance to shine (Plate 11B).

 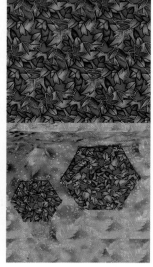

Plates 11A–B   Plates 12A–B

Plates 11A–B, Plates 12A–B: (11A) This print would be unsuitable for a large block, but the small blocks of the Diamond Ring wall quilt suit its scale; (11B) RIPPLES, a Diamond Ring wall quilt, detail; (12A) a print with a 6" repeat; (12B) smaller-scale prints show more diversity in smaller blocks.

Plate 12A shows another print with a 6" repeat. Notice how the smaller Hexagon Star

blocks show off the kaleidoscope effects to better advantage (Plate 12B). The Hybrid Lilies wall quilt and the LeMoyne Star baby or wall quilt are also good projects for smaller-scale prints.

The Background and Accent Fabrics

These fabrics should complement the main print without competing for attention with the kaleidoscope designs. Because it is hard to predict the suitability of a particular background until you see some of the kaleidoscopes, I believe in "designing on the installment plan." Whenever possible, I like to select my main print first and cut the pieces for the blocks. Then I can take a few triangles or diamonds and lay them out on various backgrounds, arranging them as if they were sewn (Plates 14A–C). Background colors that contrast strongly with the blocks will create a much different effect than colors that blend with the blocks. This contrast gives me a better idea of the effectiveness of different choices, and I often end up with something I would not have considered if I had simply piled up bolts of fabric.

If you need to select the main print and background fabric at the same time, consider how various small sections of the main print will look with different backgrounds. Try folding the end of the main fabric into a triangle shape. Lay this triangle on your background possibilities and cover the rest of the bolt to better concentrate on the effect (Plate 15, page 14). If you like it, refold the fabric to another section and check again.

Good choices for background fabrics include textural prints, marbled effects, small all-over designs with few colors, and monoprints (prints that appear to be solid colors). These subtle, low-contrast prints help to hide the seams in the background areas better than solid fabrics. Hand-dyed and mock hand-dyed fabrics offer a nice contrast to the symmetry of the kaleidoscope blocks (Plates 16A–B, page 14). Black or very dark backgrounds provide a dramatic setting for dark-ground prints. It is best to avoid stripes, plaids, and other directional fabrics in the background, as these tend to be distracting

(Plate 16C, page 14). Follow these same guidelines for the accent fabrics. If the accent fabric appears only in a straight border, you may also consider stripes. As with the background, you may want to postpone your decision until you can see the effect with the kaleidoscope blocks.

Plate 13A: HANDS ALL AROUND by the author, 1997. The fabric shown in Plate 6A was used for the center stars in this quilt and 13B.

Plate 13B: HANDS ALL AROUND by Mrs. M. L. "Hutch" Frederick, Pittsford, New York, 1997. Note how different this star looks compared to Plate 13A.

Plates 14A–C: Test cut pieces on various backgrounds.

Plate 15: Lay a folded corner of the
main print on a background fabric.

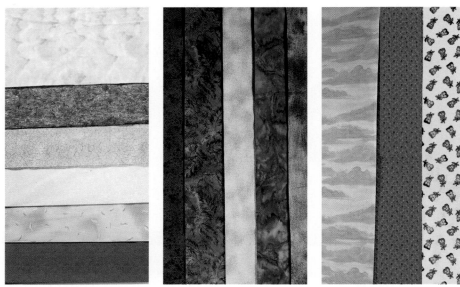

Plates 16A–C: (16A–B) Textured prints, hand-dyed fabrics and their printed imitators are good choices for background and accent fabrics; (16C) directional designs and small, busy prints may detract
from the main fabric.

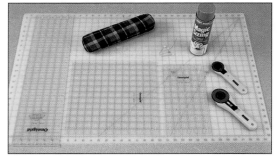

Plate 17: Essentials (rulers, mat, cutters) and some helpful
extras (seam roll, flower-head pins, fabric sizing).

Magic Props: Supplies for Stack-n-Whack Quilting

The supplies you will need for these projects
are probably already in your sewing kit. If
not, you will find them readily available at
most quilt shops or through mail-order quilt
resources (see Sources, page 111).

Here are the essentials:

The proper tools are essential to making Stack-
n-Whack magic work for you.

• Rotary cutter. The 1¾" (45mm) or larger blade is a must. The small size just will not do the job on four or more layers. Treat yourself to a new blade before you start. If you frequently need to cut multiple layers or if physical limitations such as arthritis make cutting more difficult, consider getting one of the extra-large cutters.

• Self-healing rotary cutting mat. You will want one that allows you to cut across a folded width of fabric without shifting the fabric. The 17" x 23" mat is the minimum practical size for these projects. A 24" x 36" or larger size will speed up your cutting time, and reduce the chance of damaging your tabletop if you get too enthusiastic when you cut.

• Rotary cutting rulers. Quality, precision-made rulers are a key ingredient for successful quiltmaking. There are dozens of brands and styles available, and some are better than others, especially where angle lines are concerned. Some of the projects in this book require a ruler with a 30° or 60° angle line and several use a 45° line. I have attempted to make the cutting illustrations as universal as possible, but, I confess, I have not tried every ruler on the market. You need to have a ruler that is very accurate, one in which the angle lines are well placed. It is helpful if the lines run in both directions. Rulers also need to have legible, frequently spaced ⅛" markings. These are an important asset when you are cutting triangles and diamonds, which often involve ⅛" measurements.

Keep several rulers handy and switch as you work so you can use the right-size ruler for the task. A 12" ruler is not convenient for cutting strips across the width of the fabric, and a 24" ruler is pretty awkward for cutting 2" squares. At a minimum, you will want to have a long rectangular ruler (6" x 24") with angle lines and one smaller rectangular or square ruler.

You may also find the following supplies helpful:

• Flower-head pins. I recommend using these to secure the layers for cutting, when necessary. These are long pins with a flat head that will not interfere with the ruler. If you do not have these, you can use pins with small metal heads. But watch out because these can easily disappear in your cutting area, only to ruin a cutting blade later.

• Spray sizing. Spraying your fabrics with sizing or a light spray starch and pressing them dry before you cut your pieces will make them easier to handle and help prevent stretching. Look for these products in the laundry aisle at a supermarket or chain store.

• Seam roll. This sausage-shaped, tightly padded fabric tube allows you to press seam allowances open without catching the tip of your iron on nearby allowances (Plate 18). You can create a makeshift seam roll by tightly rolling a magazine and covering it with an old hand towel, or you can look for one from a store or mail-order resource that sells dressmaking and tailoring notions.

Plate 18: Using a seam roll to press seams open.

• Pressing mat with grid. Use the grid lines to keep your blocks free from distortion, especially when you are pressing pieces with bias or off-grain edges.

• Design wall. For larger projects, a design

wall is extremely helpful. This is a vertical surface to which you can pin pieces or blocks to keep them in position until you are ready to sew them together. If you can place it where you can stand back a bit, the design wall will also help you decide on the overall arrangement of the blocks. You can improvise a design wall by tacking up a solid-color bed sheet. If you are short on wall space, a portable free-standing design wall is especially nice. You can order directions for a snap-together PVC pipe frame, along with special plastic clips to attach flannel to the frame (see Sources, page 111).

Sleight of Hand: Rotary Cutting, Piecing, and Pressing Tricks

Rotary Cutting

Nearly every magician has an assistant, and yours is your rotary cutter. The secret to the Stack-n-Whack method is in the cutting. To get the identical triangles or diamonds needed for each block, you will need to cut through a stack of fabric up to eight layers thick.

> **NOTE**
> If you separate the layers before you have cut all the pieces, you will risk distorting the kaleidoscope effect!

Even if you have done a lot of rotary cutting, please review the cutting tips below. You do not need to complete a weight-lifting program to cut multiple layers. Here are some suggestions from a "98-pound weakling:"

• If you cut left-handed, you may find the whacking illustrations easier to follow if you rotate the page counterclockwise a quarter or one-half turn, so that the cutter appears to the left of the ruler.

• The cutter blade should be facing the ruler, whether you cut right- or left-handed.

• Keep the cutter at about a 45° angle to the mat (Figure 1-1A). If the angle is too low, the safety shield will interfere with cutting (Figure 1-1B); if it is too high, it will be more difficult to control and potentially dangerous (Figure 1-1C).

Figures 1-1A–C: (1A) Correct angle, (1B) angle too low, (1C) angle too high.

• It is best to stand up when cutting multiple layers, so you can use your body weight for leverage. Cut with your whole arm, not just your wrist. The motion should begin at the shoulder and flow smoothly. Avoid sawing back and forth, which will result in jagged edges. If you are not cutting all the layers in one motion, try using more pressure. If the blade is skipping, leaving threads uncut every few inches, it has a nick. Put in a new blade.

• Always cut away from your body. It is too easy to be hurt if you cut toward yourself. If the cutting angle is awkward, rearrange the fabric, turn the mat, or if possible, walk around the table so that you can cut safely.

• If you have trouble keeping the ruler from sliding, try placing your pinkie over the edge of the ruler, opposite the cutting side. You can also purchase small dots or squares of adhesive sandpaper to attach to your ruler.

• Close the safety shield when you set down the cutter! If you are not already in the habit, keep after yourself until it is second nature. This is a common-sense safety precaution, and it will also extend the life of your blades.

• A blade that rolls stiffly may be gummed up with oil and lint. Take the cutter apart and wipe the blade and holder clean. When you reassemble a cutter after cleaning or changing the blade, do not tighten the nut more than necessary. The blade should turn freely so that you and the cutter are not overworked.

• There are many styles of rotary cutters on the market, and some types may work better for you than others. If you are having irreconcilable differences with the one you are using, look at other styles and try some out if possible. The extra-large cutters are worth checking out, too, especially if hand strength is a problem for you. These cut multiple layers with minimum effort.

• Mats with grids are handy for measuring oversized pieces, but try using your rulers to square off fabric and measure narrower strips. This can save time and increase accuracy, since you are measuring the fabric and holding it securely with the ruler as you cut.

• If you need to cut large triangles, such as the setting triangles used for the Kaleidoscope Pinwheel quilts, you may find that your ruler will not reach from corner to corner when you are cutting the square on the diagonal. To get around this problem, press the square in half on the diagonal in both directions, then unfold the square and cut on the pressed fold lines.

• Whenever possible, use more than one edge or angle line of the ruler to increase accuracy. For example, when you are cutting a square into two half-square triangles, you could cut a diagonal line from corner to corner, using the ruler simply as a straightedge. But a more accurate way to do this is to line up the 45° line of the ruler on one edge of the square and place the ruler from corner to corner (Figure 1-2). Using this method, you will also find out quickly if your square is really square. This can save many headaches later on. This concept be-

comes even more important when cutting diamonds, since cockeyed angles can quickly sabotage your piecing efforts.

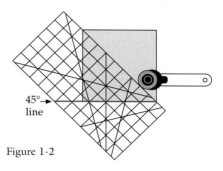

45°
line

Figure 1-2

• You can sometimes use two rulers together for large measurements. For instance, if you need to cut a 10" strip, you can place a 6" x 12" ruler with the 4" line on the cut edge, and butt a 6" x 24" ruler up next to the shorter ruler (Figure 1-3). Cut along the edge of the long ruler.

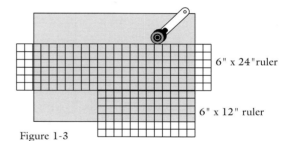

6" x 24" ruler

6" x 12" ruler

Figure 1-3

• If you have trouble seeing or remembering where to place the ruler for a repetitive measurement, use a strip of masking tape or ¼" quilter's tape on the ruler to clearly mark your place. Remove the tape when you are finished cutting so it will not leave a residue on the ruler.

• Measure twice, whack once!

Machine Piecing

• Always maintain an accurate ¼" seam allowance. When I started quilting, I thought the seam allowance was not that critical as long as I kept it a consistent size. While this theory may hold true for simple blocks like

Nine Patches, it definitely does not apply to blocks that have diagonal lines meeting at the center. Those diagonal seam lines seem to direct all the problems to the middle, and you may end up with a block that pouches up in the center. True ¼" presser feet are available for almost all sewing machines, and they are well worth the investment. To check the accuracy of your seam allowance, cut three 2"-wide strips of fabric. Sew these together and measure the total width of the sewn unit. It should be 5". If it is not, try again, adjusting the width of the seam allowance until you get a 5" unit. Then mark your needle plate with a permanent marker or use a seam guide.

• Match pieces at the beginning and end of the seam and keep the pieces together. If you find that one piece ends up longer than the other, pin or hold the bottom edges together securely and ease the seam as you sew.

• As you piece, be sure to keep the pieces feeding straight toward the needle at the beginning and end of the seam. Careening off at the tips is a common habit that contributes to piecing headaches.

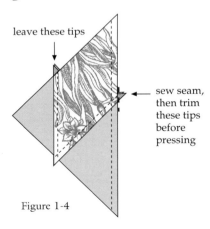

leave these tips

sew seam, then trim these tips before pressing

Figure 1-4

• When you are joining two pieced units, try using the "dog ears" (the triangle tips that stick out past the seam allowance) to help match up seams. I never trim these until I have sewn the seam. By cutting both sets of triangle tips at

once, I reduce my trimming time by half. Snip them off with scissors or a rotary cutter just before you press the seam (Figure 1-4).

• To match seams that cross, try using a "positioning" pin. Push the positioning pin through one block unit, from the wrong side, exactly where the seam allowances cross from the previous sewing step. Then, push the pin through the same point on the other block unit. Squeeze the two units together at the pin (Figure 1-5A). Hold the pin perpendicular to the fabric; do not bring it back up through the fabric. Place another pin about ¼" away from the positioning pin. Pin this one flat against the fabric as you normally would. Use a third pin on the other side of the matching point. Remove the positioning pin and sew the seam (Figure 1-5B). Remove the remaining pins just before the presser foot reaches them, or "walk" your machine over the pins one stitch at a time.

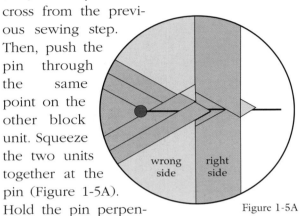

wrong side right side

Figure 1-5A

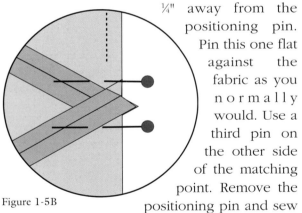

Figure 1-5B

• You do not always need to pin. If you can get accurate results by holding and guiding the fabric with your fingers, go for it! When six or eight seams come together in the center of a block, I usually use a positioning pin as described previously. For simpler seams, I often use the "peek and pinch" method. To do this, sew down the seam until you are about 2" from the matching point. Stop with the needle in the fabric. Lift the top piece a bit so that you can see the match point on both pieces and bring them together. Pinch them against the needle plate with your forefinger until you get past the seam. With practice, you can get quite good at this. You can also try this method using a pin instead of your finger, poking just the tip through the match points and using the shaft of the pin to guide the seam toward the needle as you sew.

Pressing

• Before cutting your pieces, spray the fabric with sizing or spray starch and press until dry. This will help prevent the pieces from stretching as you sew.

• Use a dry iron during block construction and be especially careful when pressing bias edges so that you don't stretch them. I use the grid on my pressing mat to make sure my pieces stay true. If a piece begins to distort, I can line up the straight edges with the grid and use a bit of steam to ease it back into shape.

• Here's a technique for pressing seam allowances quickly. If you want to press the seam allowance toward the darker patch, lay the sewn unit on the ironing board with the darker patch on top. Use the tip of the iron to flip the darker patch up. Press the unit flat, using just the tip of the iron along the seam line to smooth out any pleats that might start to develop.

• While pressing seams to one side is a standard quilting rule, I have found that it helps me get a more accurate center and a flatter block if I press open those seams that will come together in the center. If you have trouble pressing allowances open without catching the tip of the iron in other seams, try using a seam roll. The seam you are pressing lies on the top of the roll, and the rest of the fabric falls down the sides, out of the way of the iron (Plate 18, page 15).

Chapter Two

Stacking the Deck:
The Magician's Secret Revealed

Stack-n-Whack for Kaleidoscope Effects

All the designs in this book begin with the same procedure for preparing (stacking) and cutting (whacking) the fabrics. Once you have learned this method for one design, you will be able to apply it to all the others, using the number of layers and specific measurements given for each design in Chapters 3 through 7.

What follows is an overview of the method. The photos show the transition of one fabric from yardage to blocks, in this case, the Hexagon Star blocks.

STACK

1. Cut a rectangle of the main fabric to the size given in your project for the guide piece.

2. Use the guide piece for cutting identical repeats. The number of repeats needed depends on the number of identical pieces in the block. For example, a LeMoyne Star block requires eight repeats, and a Hexagon Star block requires six.

3. Layer the repeats so that all the motifs in the print line up through the stack. Pin the repeats together for accurate cutting.

WHACK!

1. Using the directions for your project, cut strips from the repeats, cutting through all the layers at once. If you separate the layers, you will lose the kaleidoscope effect.

2. Cut the stacked strips into the units needed for the block, either triangles or diamonds. Each stack contains the identical pieces needed for one block, called a block kit. Pin each block kit together and set aside for piecing.

Read through the directions that follow before cutting your main fabric. The stacking directions are the same for all designs. The whacking directions vary, depending on the shape used in the design.

Finding the Fabric Repeats

In the Stack-n-Whack chart for each quilt pattern, you will find the width for the guide piece. The length of the guide piece will usually be one lengthwise design repeat. This figure will depend on your print (see About Design Repeats, page 11).

The repeats are cut from a single layer of fabric. To make a guide piece for cutting the repeats, measure across the fabric, from selvage to selvage, and use a snip to mark the width of the guide piece given in the chart for your project. At the snip, tear or cut along the lengthwise grain for about a yard. Fold the extra fabric out of the way. Square off the end of the guide piece section (Plate 19).

Switch the bulk of the fabric to your right if you are right-handed (or to your left if you are left-handed). Then smooth out the squared-off end of the fabric on your cutting mat.

Now, you will need to determine your fabric design repeat length. Examine the selvage of your fabric near the squared-off end and find a motif close to the edge. Mark the beginning of the motif with a pin. Move your eyes along the selvage until you find the same motif, in the same orientation. Mark the beginning of this motif with another pin. Measure between the pins to find the design repeat (Plate 20). Check the Stack-n-Whack chart for your project to see how many design repeats to use for the length of the guide piece.

Remove the pins and measure, from the cut edge, along each side to the length you have established for the guide piece. Mark the length with rotary cuts (Plate 21). Line up your ruler with the cut marks and cut across the width to make the guide piece (Plate 22, page 22). This guide piece is the key to cutting identical layers of fabric, so that you can cut the matching pieces needed for each block in one operation, making efficient use of time and fabric.

With selvages and cut edges aligned, lay the guide piece on the remaining fabric so that the print matches exactly. Smooth out the guide piece and use your fingertips to match up the design all across the cut edge that is nearest to the remaining uncut fabric. The edge should nearly disappear as it lines up with the print on the lower, uncut layer (Plate 23). When you have matched it exactly, pin the two layers together with flat flower-head pins

Plate 19: Fold the remaining fabric out of the way and square off the cut end. (This single layer of fabric has been torn to the needed width.)

Plate 20: Mark the beginning and end of one repeat with pins. Measure between the pins to find the repeat length.

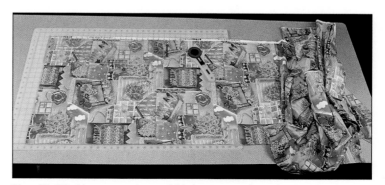

Plate 21: Working on one layer of fabric, measure from the straightened edge and mark the guide-piece length. See the Stack-n-Whack chart for your project to find the number of repeat lengths to use for the guide piece.

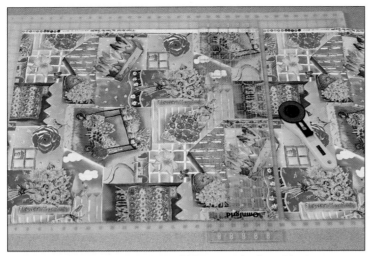

Plate 22: Cut across the single layer of fabric to make the guide piece.

cut edge

Plate 23: Lay the guide piece on the remaining length of fabric and match up the design at the cut edge with the layer below. (The edge nearly disappears.)

(see supplies list, page 14) or silk pins. Lay your ruler down along the pinned edge and cut across (Plate 24). You now have two identical print rectangles (Plate 25).

Unpin the layers and set the newly cut piece aside. Cut or tear along the length of the fabric, if necessary, for the next piece. Smooth out the portion you are cutting. Use the guide piece again to cut the third repeat. Unpin it and set it with the second.

Repeat this process until you have the necessary number of repeats (Plate 26). Include the guide piece in the total. Be sure to cut all these repeats from the same half of the fabric. Printing and finishing processes can cause slight distortions even in high quality fabrics, and the differences may be noticeable in the finished blocks if you use crosswise, rather than lengthwise, repeats.

Stacking the Layers

You now have four to eight identical layers in your first set of repeats. One at a time, take the layers and press them lightly. If you have prewashed the fabric, you may want to use a little sizing or spray starch to return some crispness to the fabric, which will make the pieces easier to handle and will help keep bias edges from stretching.

Stack the layers, smoothing out each piece so that the selvages and cut edges line up. When you have all the layers stacked, you can use a method I call "stick-pinning" to position them accurately. You will need a few flower-head pins and one pin with a large round head.

To "stick-pin" fabric layers, select a point on the fabric design about 2" in from the selvages and 2" to 3" from the cut edge. Look for something that is distinctive and easy to spot. In Plate 27 (page 24), I have used the corner of a brown box. Place the tip of the round-headed pin on this spot. Lift the top layer of fabric, sliding the tip of the pin through. Find the same point on the next layer and slide the pin through. Continue lifting layers and pinning through this spot until you have gone through all the layers. Slide the pin all the way through to the head and hold it in place with your thumb and forefinger. Hold the pin straight vertically and smooth out the surrounding fabric. Take a flower-head pin and pin across through all the layers, right beside the stick pin (Plate 28, page 24). Remove the stick pin. Lay the fabric down flat and repeat the pinning at three other points across the width. The extra time spent in careful pinning now will pay off later in more accurate blocks.

Once you have stacked the layers, continue with the whacking directions for your project. Plates 29 through 35 on pages 25–27 follow a Hexagon Star throw quilt project through the cutting steps. Notice that the sewn hexagons in Plate 36, page 27, look a little different from the cut pieces, because part of the print is in the seam allowances. The finished quilt, Summer Bouquets, appears in Plate 49, page 72.

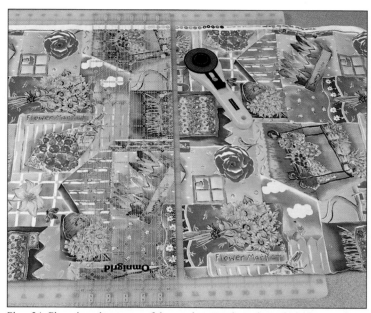

Plate 24: Place the ruler on top of the two layers and cut through the bottom layer.

Plate 25: Remove the pins. You now have two print rectangles. Set one aside.

Plate 26: Use the guide piece to cut additional identical repeats, until you have the number required for your project.

Plate 27: Pin down through all the layers, matching a point in the motif on each layer.

Stack-n-Whack Again

For some projects, you will need to cut a second set of repeats for additional block kits. Cut a second guide piece from the remaining width of fabric. It should not be identical to the first guide piece, since you will want these block kits to be different from the first set. If the print you are using has side-by-side repeats across the width, trim off a couple of inches before measuring and cutting the second guide piece so that it will not begin and end in exactly the same place. If your project calls for a third guide piece, this one should also be different from the first two.

Now that you have learned the secret, it is time to make your own magic. On with the show!

Plate 28: Hold the stick pin vertically and use a flower-head pin to secure the layers. Remove the stick pin. Repeat several times across the width.

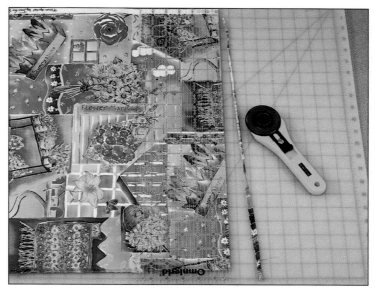

Plate 29: Trim the pinned stack.

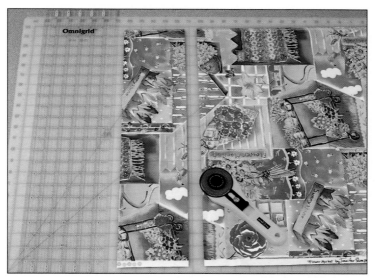

Plate 30: Turn the stack around or rotate the mat. Using the whacking directions and measurements for your project, cut a strip set through all the layers.

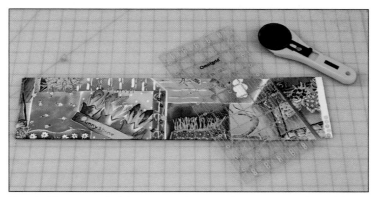

Plate 31: Trim one end of the strip set. This photo shows the 60° angle used for the Hexagon Star projects.

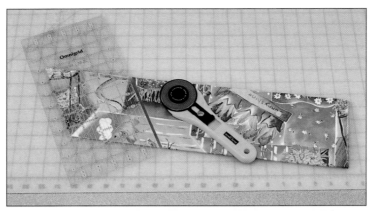

Plate 32: Turn the strip set or rotate the mat. Cut the shapes needed for your project.

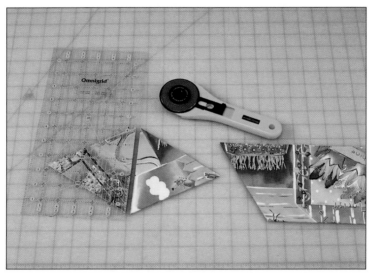

Plate 33: The diamond shape is cut into 60° triangles for the Hexagon Star block. Each stack of triangles is a "block kit."

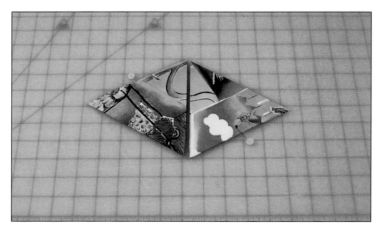

Plate 34: Pin each block kit.

Plate 35: Each block kit contains a set of identical pieces for one block.

Plate 36: Use a few block kits to select a background fabric. For a full view of the finished quilt, see Plate 49 on page 72.

Chapter Three
Half-Square Triangle Magic

Plate 37: STAINED GLASS by author, 1996. A black background sets off the 18 jewel-toned blocks in this queen-sized quilt. (Pattern instructions begin on facing page.)

Cutting Main Fabric A

Follow the directions for whacking half-square triangles, beginning on page 29. If you have not chosen the background fabric yet, you can preview various background fabrics by arranging a few of the block kits on each one.

Stack-n-Whack Chart for Kaleidoscope Pinwheel Queen Quilt			
Guide Piece...	**Stack...**	**Whack...**	**To Make...**
21" wide x one full repeat long*	8 identical repeats of Main Fabric A**	(3) 6¼" x 21" strips	18 half-square triangle block kits (6 per strip)
* For fabrics with a repeat under 13", use two full repeats for length of guide piece. **For fabrics with a repeat under 20", you may need two stacks of eight.			

Cutting Background Fabric B – Throw Quilt			
Position in Quilt	**First Cut**	**Second Cut**	**Third Cut**
Side Setting Triangles	(2) 22½" strips across width	(2) 22½" squares	Cut twice on the diagonal to make 6 side triangles (with 2 left over)
Corner Setting Triangles	(2) 12" squares from remainder of 22½" strips above	Cut once on the diagonal to make 4 corner triangles	
Block Triangles	(3) 6¼" strips across width	(16) 6¼" squares	Cut once on the diagonal to make 32 half-square triangles
Block Rectangles	(8) 2¾" strips across width	(32) 2¾" x 8½" rectangles	

Cutting Background Fabric B – Queen Quilt

Position in Quilt	First Cut	Second Cut	Third Cut
Side Setting Triangles	(3) 22½" strips across width	(3) 22½" squares	Cut twice on the diagonal to make 10 side triangles (with 2 left over)
Corner Setting Triangles	(2) 12" squares from remainder of 22½" strips above	Cut once on the diagonal to make 4 half-square triangles	
Block Triangles	(6) 6¼" strips across width	(36) 6¼" squares	Cut once on the diagonal to make 72 half-square triangles
Block Rectangles	(18) 2¾" strips across width	(72) 2¾" x 8½" rectangles	

Piecing the Pinwheel Blocks

Piece 8 blocks for throw/ *18 for queen.*

1. Divide the block kit (eight identical triangles) into two piles of four triangles. Place the piles next to your machine with the short side of the triangle on the right as shown in Figure 3-5. Take a Fabric A triangle from the first stack and sew a background triangle to the right edge. Have the background triangle on top as you sew (Figure 3-6A). Press the seam allowances toward Fabric A (Figure 3-6B). Repeat with the remaining three triangles in the first stack.

2. Add the rectangles of background fabric to the other stack of four Main Fabric A triangles, lining up the top and right-hand edges. The background rectangle should be on top as you sew (Figure 3-7A). Sew just past the tip of the Fabric A triangle. Press the seam allowances toward Main Fabric A (Figure 3-7B).

3. Lay the triangle/rectangle unit (from Step 2) next to a triangle/triangle unit (from Step 1), to see how they will be joined (Figure 3-8A). Lay the triangle/triangle unit on top of the other unit, rights sides together. The rectangle extends beyond the triangle. Sew with a ¼" allowance (Figure 3-8B). Trim extra fabric from the rectangle, leaving a ¼" seam allowance. Press allowance open (Figure 3-8C). Repeat with the other triangle units to make four quarter-blocks.

4. Join a pair of quarter-blocks, right sides together, to make a half-block. After sewing the units, make sure seams intersect ¼" from the edge at the center of the block, and adjust the seam if necessary. Clip the tips along the seam allowance (Figure 3-9A). Press allowances open (Figure 3-9B). Repeat for the other half-block.

5. Sew the half-blocks together, matching the center seams. Press the seam allowances open (Figure 3-10).

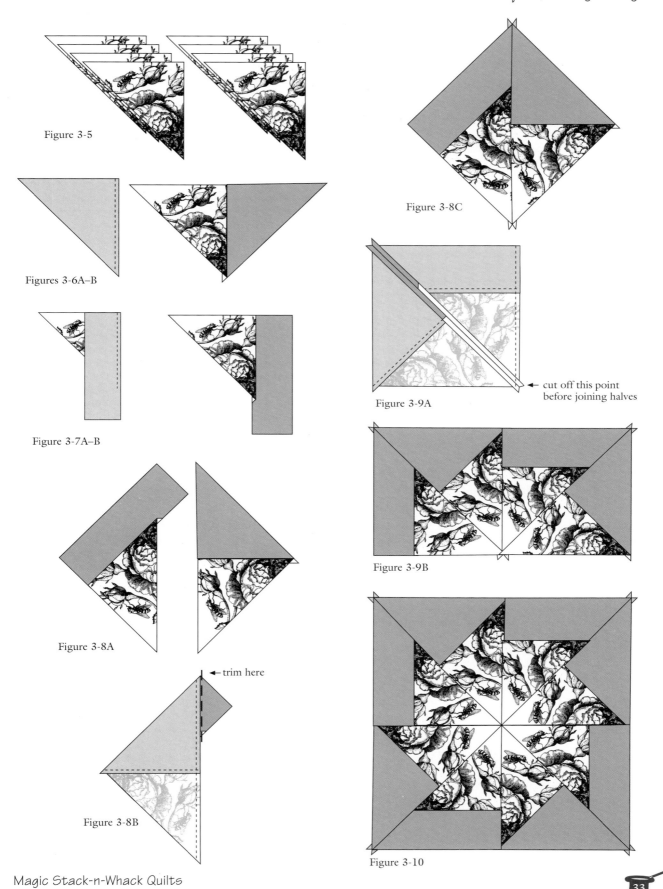

Figure 3-5

Figures 3-6A–B

Figure 3-7A–B

Figure 3-8A

← trim here

Figure 3-8B

Figure 3-8C

← cut off this point
before joining halves

Figure 3-9A

Figure 3-9B

Figure 3-10

Assembling the Quilt

Lay out the quilt according to the appropriate quilt assembly diagram, pages 39 or 40. Sew the blocks into diagonal rows, then sew the rows together. Using a rotary cutter and a long ruler, trim any extra fabric from the side and corner triangles before adding the borders.

Adding Borders – Throw Quilt	
Fabric and Position	**Cut**
Accent Fabric C – Border 1	(6) 1½" strips across width
Main Fabric A – Border 2	(4) 3½" strips x 67" cut lengthwise or (6) 3½" strips across width

Adding Borders – Queen Quilt	
Fabric and Position	**Cut**
Accent Fabric C – Borders 1 and 3	(17) 2½" strips across width
Main Fabric A – Border 2	(9) 6½" strips across width or (2) 6½" x 93" strips and (2) 6½" x 84" strips cut lengthwise

1. Both borders have butted corners. For border 1, piece the Fabric C strips together into one long strip. Measure the quilt top down the center and cut two borders this length from the strip. Sew the borders to the long sides. Measure across the width in the center of the quilt, including borders, and cut two borders this length. Sew them to the top and bottom.

2. Add border 2 in the same manner, piecing the strips first if you cut them across the width.

3. For the queen, repeat Step 1 with the remainder of the Accent Fabric C strip.

Finishing the Quilt

See Chapter Eight for suggestions on quilting design and binding. Prepare the backing by piecing together two 1⅞-yard lengths of backing fabric/*two 3¼-yard lengths for queen.* Layer, quilt, and bind.

Pinwheel Plus Wall Quilt

STACKED DECK

See Plate 40, page 36   Finished Quilt: 50" x 50"
Skill Level: Easy   Finished Block: 15" (9 blocks)

Cutting Main Fabric A

See page 29 for yardage. Follow the directions for whacking half-square triangles on page 20. Choose nine of the block kits for the quilt. (You will have extras.) If you have not chosen the background fabric yet, arrange a few of the kits on various fabrics and select one.

Stack-n-Whack Chart for Pinwheel Plus Wall Quilt

Guide Piece...	Stack...	Whack...	To Make...
21" wide x one full repeat long*	8 identical repeats of Main Fabric A	(2) 6¼" x 21" strips	9 half-square triangle block kits (6 per strip; you have 3 extras)
*For fabrics with a repeat under 13", you will need a second stack; cut one strip from each stack.			

Cutting Fabrics B, C, and D – Pinwheel Plus Wall Quilt

Position in Quilt	First Cut	Second Cut	Third Cut
Background Fabric B Block Triangles	(3) 6¼" strips across width	(18) 6¼" squares	Cut once on the diagonal to make 36 half-square triangles
Background Fabric B Block Rectangles	(9) 2¾" strips across width	(36) 2¾" x 8½" rectangles	
Background Fabric B Inner Border	(7) 2¾" strips across width	(8) 2¾" x 15½" rectangles, and (8) 2¾" x 11" rectangles	
Accent Fabric C Block Accent Triangles	(8) 2¾" strips across width	(104) 2¾" squares (13 per strip)	
Accent Fabric D Outer Border	(6) 2¾" strips across width	(8) 2¾" x 15½" rectangles, and (8) 2¾" x 14" rectangles	

(Clockwise from top left) Plate 38: JANUARY THAW by author, 1994. The Kaleidoscope Pinwheel Throw is a quick and easy project for beginners. The "blades" appear to spin like a child's whirligig. (Pattern instructions begin on page 29.)

Plate 39: OLD GLORY KALEIDOSCOPE PINWHEEL by John M. Teasley, Superior, WI, 1997. Machine quilted by Debra A. Lussier, Superior, WI. This twin-sized quilt was the 13-year-old boy's fourth quilting project.

Plate 40: STACKED DECK by author, 1996. A novelty casino print creates blocks that spin like roulette wheels. Pattern instructions begin on page 35.)

Piecing the Pinwheel Plus Blocks

Piece eight blocks, following the illustrated instructions below.

1. To mark the stitching line for the accent triangles, press each Fabric C square in half once on the diagonal, right side out.

2. Unfold a C square and place it at the right-angle corner on top of a B triangle, right sides together, and stitch as shown (Figure 3-11A). Trim the seam allowance to ¼" and press open the C triangle (Figure 3-11B). Repeat for each B triangle.

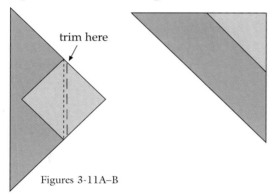

Figures 3-11A–B

3. Lay a C square on one end of a B rectangle, right sides together. Stitch on the fold line from the upper left corner of the square to the lower right corner of the square and rectangle (Figure 3-12A). Trim seam allowances to ¼" and press the C triangle open (Figure 3-12B). Repeat for each B rectangle.

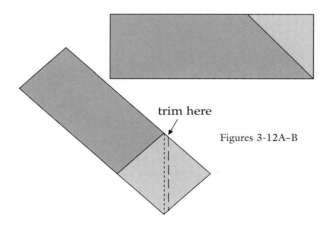

Figures 3-12A–B

4. Follow Steps 1 and 2 of the pinwheel block instructions (page 32), placing the accent triangles at the right-angle corners of Main Fabric A triangles (Figures 3-13A through 3-14B). Finish the block, following Steps 3 through 5 (Figures 3-8A through 3-10 on page 33).

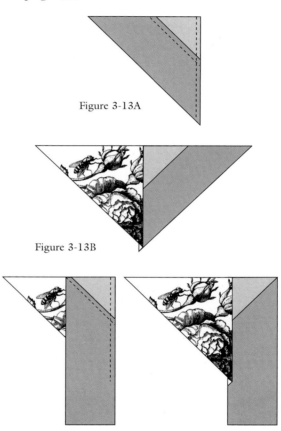

Figure 3-13A

Figure 3-13B

Figures 3-14A–B

Assembling the Quilt

1. Pin the blocks to a design wall or lay them out on the floor as shown in the quilt assembly diagram on page 40 and decide on the block arrangement.

2. Sew the vertical seams in each row, then sew the horizontal rows together.

3. For the inner border, sew a Fabric C square to one end of each 2¾" x 11" Fabric

B rectangle. On four of these rectangles, the seam should go from the upper-left corner of the square to the lower-right corner (Figures 3-15A–B). On the other four rectangles, the seam should go from the upper-right corner of the square to the lower-left corner (Figures 3-16A–B).

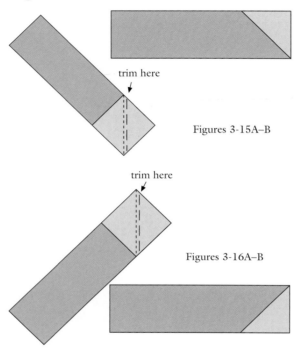

trim here

Figures 3-15A–B

trim here

Figures 3-16A–B

4. Sew C squares to each end of the 2¾" x 15½" rectangles of Background Fabric B (Figure 3-17A). The seam should go from the upper-left corner of the square to the lower-right corner of the square and rectangle on one end. On the other end, the seam should go from the upper-right corner of the square and rectangle to the lower-left corner of the square. Trim the allowances and press the C triangles open (Figure 3-17B).

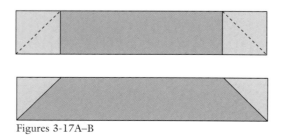

Figures 3-17A–B

5. Sew together four border strips as shown in the Pinwheel Plus Wall Quilt Assembly diagram, page 40. There is an 11" rectangle at each end with two 15½" rectangles in between.

6. Repeat steps 3 through 5 with the outer border rectangles, substituting the 16" rectangles for the 11" rectangles.

7. Sew border strips together in pairs, matching the accent fabric seams to form squares. The outer border extends beyond the inner border to allow for mitering corners. Mark the dots on the inner-border allowances, as shown in the assembly diagram, to aid in matching block seams to border seams.

8. Pin the borders to one side at a time, matching the dots on the 15½" rectangles with the seams between the blocks. Stitch, beginning and ending at the outer marks in the corners.

9. To miter the borders, lay the corner of the quilt flat on your ironing surface with one border overlapping the adjacent border, right sides together. Fold under the excess fabric at the end of the top border strip at a 45° angle. The edges of the excess border strips should line up. Adjust them so the seams match; press. Lift the top layer carefully while holding the pressed fold in place and pin through the two layers of border fabric near the fold. Fold the quilt on the diagonal, right sides together. Keeping the rest of the quilt out of the way, stitch along the pressed fold line from the inner corner to the outer edge. Check the right side to make sure the seams match and the miter lies flat, then trim the seam allowance on the mitered seam to ¼" and press open. Repeat for the other corners.

Finishing the Quilt

See Chapter Eight for suggestions on quilting design and binding. Prepare the backing by piecing together two 1⅝-yard lengths of backing fabric. Layer, quilt, and bind.

Kaleidoscope Pinwheel
Queen Quilt Assembly

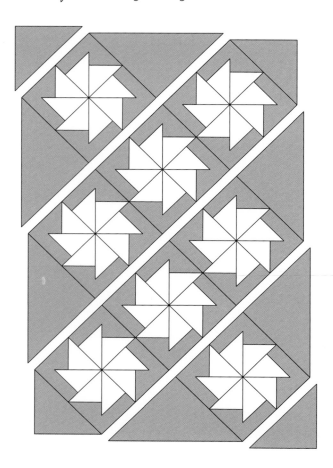

Kaleidoscope Pinwheel
Throw Quilt Assembly

Pinwheel Plus
Wall Quilt
Assembly

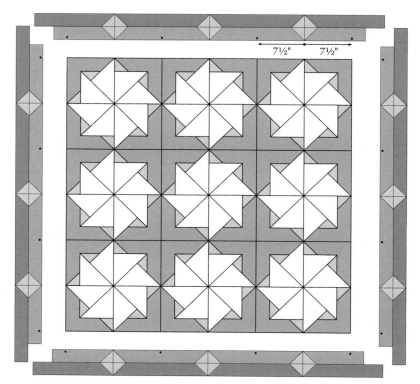

7½"   7½"

Color Key	
□	Main Fabric A
▨	Background Fabric B
▨	Accent Fabric C
▨	Border Fabric D

Chapter Four
45° Triangle Magic

Plate 41: RIPPLES by author, 1997. This wall quilt has 6" blocks that work well with smaller repeat fabrics. What a wonderful wedding or anniversary gift. (Pattern instructions begin on page 42.)

Diamond Ring Wall Quilt

RIPPLES
See plate 41, page 41
Skill Level: Advanced Intermediate
Finished Quilt: 42" x 42"
Finished Block: 6" (49 blocks)

Diamond Ring Queen Quilt

48 PARROT DIAMOND RING
See plate 42, page 50
Skill Level: Advanced Intermediate
Finished Quilt: 90" x 90"
Finished Block: 10" (81 blocks)

This chapter's projects are easy to make, if you follow the directions carefully. Since the kaleidoscope effect extends past the boundaries of each block into the adjacent blocks, it is important to piece the blocks in order.

The 22½° angle for this triangle is an odd angle, which you will not find on a standard rotary cutting ruler, so we have provided a "double-triangle" cutting guide for these projects. The double triangle, when cut in half diagonally, makes two 45° triangles.

Whacking Main Fabric Triangles for the Block Kits

1. Prepare the cutting guide on page 107, for the block size you are using, in one of the following ways: Trace the guide as accurately as possible on clear template plastic. Cut out the plastic cutting guide. With clear tape, attach the cutting guide to the underside of your ruler, with the right edge of the guide aligned with the right edge of the ruler (Figure 4-1). Or, you can lay your ruler over the plastic cutting guide with the right edge of the ruler over the right edge of the cutting guide. Mark the guidelines on the ruler with a permanent marker or tape. (Use permanent marker so it doesn't rub off on your fabric.)

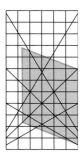

Figure 4-1

2. Refer to the Stack-n-Whack chart for your project to determine the size of the fabric guide piece needed. Using the basic stacking method, page 20, cut and stack eight identical repeats of Main Fabric A.

Fabric Requirements
(Measurements are in yards unless otherwise indicated.)

If the design repeat of Main Fabric A is		6"–10"	11"–14"	15"–20"	21"–27"	over 27"
You will need this many yards	Wall	2½	3½	5	6¾	8 repeats
	Queen	6	6½	7¾	6¾	8 repeats

Additional Fabrics	Wall	Queen
Ring Fabric B	1	3⅛
Border Fabric C	1⅜	3⅜
Backing	3	8¼
Binding (cut 2½" strips crosswise)	½	¾

3. Trim about ¼" from the pinned edge of the fabric stack, if necessary, to get a smooth edge. Cut a strip through all eight layers, using the width given in the Stack-n-Whack chart. Figure 4-2 shows how to cut a 6" strip.

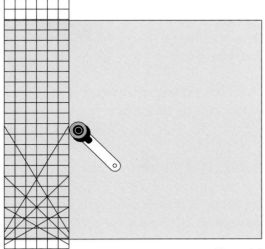

Figure 4-2

4. Lay the ruler with the cutting guide down on the strip set, with the top and bottom edges of the guide aligned with the edges of the strip (Figure 4-3). Place the edge of the ruler far enough in to avoid the selvages. Cut along the edge through all layers. Set aside this first cut. This is scrap fabric.

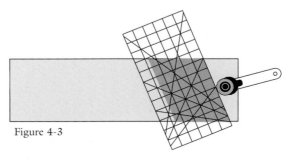

Figure 4-3

5. Carefully turn the strip set around so the angled edge is to your left (or to your right if you are left-handed). Lay the ruler down with the left edge of the cutting guide on the

Stack-n-Whack Chart for Diamond Ring Wall Quilt			
Guide Piece...	**Stack...**	**Whack...**	**To Make...**
21" wide x one full repeat long	8 identical repeats of Main Fabric A	(2) 4" x 21" strips	(20) 45° triangle block kits (10 per strip)
For fabrics with a repeat under 8", you will need a second stack; cut one strip from each stack.			

Stack-n-Whack Chart for Diamond Ring Queen Quilt			
Guide Piece...	**Stack...**	**Whack...**	**To Make...**
21" wide x one full repeat long*	8 identical repeats of Main Fabric A	(6) 6" x 21" strips	(38) 45° triangle block kits (7 per strip)
You will need two stacks of eight; cut three strips from each stack. * For fabrics with a repeat under 9", use three full repeats for length of guide piece. For fabrics with a repeat 9"–18", use two full repeats for length of guide piece.			

angled edge (Figure 4-4). Continue cutting double-triangles with the cutting guide.

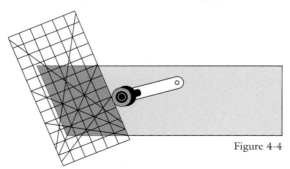

Figure 4-4

6. Line up the 45° line of your ruler with the cut edge of the piece and cut diagonally (Figure 4-5). This cut makes two block kits (Figure 4-6). Set them aside. Continue cutting the block kits from the strip, removing the pins in the stack as

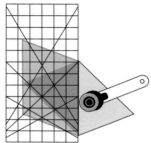

Figure 4-5

Figure 4-6

you go to avoid damaging your blade. You may be able to get an extra kit at the end of the strip by cutting a partial double-triangle (Figure 4-7).

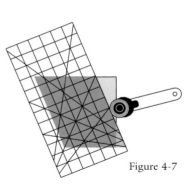

Figure 4-7

7. Continue cutting more strips until you have the number of block kits required for your project.

Whacking Ring and Border Triangles

Ring Fabric B triangles (for the "rings" around the blocks) and Border Fabric C triangles are not cut from identical repeats. Fold the fabric in half lengthwise, selvage to selvage, and cut the strip width according to the project directions. Unfold and stack the strips and cut them into triangles, following Steps 4 through 6. You do not need to pin these in sets, just stack them.

Cutting Fabrics B and C – Wall Quilt			
Fabric	**First Cut**	**Second Cut**	**Third Cut**
Ring Fabric B	(4) 4" strips across width	(36) double triangles, using 4" cutting guide (10 per strip)	Cut once on the diagonal to make (72) 45° triangles
Ring Fabric B	(5) 2¾" strips across width	(72) 2¾" squares	Cut once on the diagonal to make 144 half-square triangles
Border Fabric C	(9) 4" strips across width	(82) double triangles, using 4" cutting guide (10 per strip)	Cut once on the diagonal to make (164) 45° triangles
Border Fabric C	(2) 2¾" strips across width	(26) 2¾" squares	Cut once on the diagonal to make 52 half-square triangles

Cutting Fabrics B and C – Queen Quilt			
Fabric	**First Cut**	**Second Cut**	**Third Cut**
Ring Fabric B	(10) 6" strips across width	(64) double triangles, using 6" cutting guide (7 per strip)	Cut once on the diagonal to make (128) 45° triangles
Ring Fabric B	(13) 3⅞" strips across width	(128) 3⅞" squares	Cut once on the diagonal to make 256 half-square triangles
Border Fabric C	(16) 6" strips across width	(110) double triangles, using 6" cutting guide (7 per strip)	Cut once on the diagonal to make (220) 45° triangles
Border Fabric C	(4) 3⅞" strips across width	(34) 3⅞" squares	Cut once on the diagonal to make 68 half-square triangles

Piecing the Diamond Ring Blocks

There are three different types of blocks in the Diamond Ring quilts: the A blocks, which have eight wedges of Main Fabric A; the B blocks, which have wedges of Main Fabric A and wedges of at least one other fabric; and the C blocks, which have eight wedges of Border Fabric C. The ringed-diamond effect is achieved by piecing the A blocks and arranging them in a checkerboard pattern, then filling in around the A blocks with the remaining pieces.

Piecing the A Blocks

1. Place the block kit (eight identical triangles) next to your machine with the short edge at the top (Figure 4-8). Take the first two triangles of the set and place them right sides together.

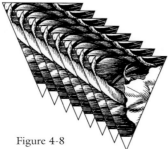
Figure 4-8

Sew these triangles together (Figure 4-9A). Repeat with three more pairs of triangles. Press allowances open (Figure 4-9B).

Figures 4-9A–B

2. Stitch two pairs together, from the outer edge to the center (Figure 4-10A). Repeat with the other two pairs. Clip triangle tips from the allowances at the block's center. Press the allowances open (Figure 4-10B). You should have two identical halves.

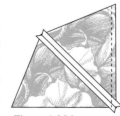
Figure 4-10A

Figure 4-10B

3. Place the halves right sides together and stitch across the center of the block, matching the crossed seams at the center. Clip the triangle tips at the center. Press allowances open to complete an octagon (Figure 4-11).

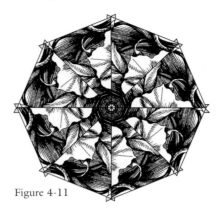

Figure 4-11

4. Add Ring Fabric B corner triangles, centering them on the wedge triangles as shown in Figure 4-12A. Press the allowances toward the corner triangles (Figure 4-12B).

Figure 4-12A

Figure 4-12B

5. Piece 13 A blocks for the wall quilt/*25 for the queen*. Save the remaining block kits for the B blocks.

Sewing the Quarter-Block Units and Piecing the C Blocks

The B and C blocks are made from quarter-block units.

1. Sew together 72 pairs of Border Fabric C wedges for the wall quilt/*96 pairs for the queen* (Figure 4-13A).

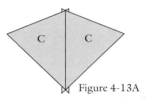

Figure 4-13A

2. Divide each remaining block kit into two sets of four wedges. You will need 13 sets of four for the wall quilt/*25 sets for the queen* (you will have an extra set). Sew a Ring Fabric B wedge to each Fabric A wedge, with Fabric A on the left as shown in Figure 4-13B. Keep the identical sets of four together.

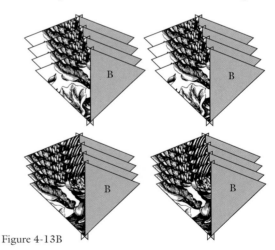

Figure 4-13B

3. Sew together the 20 pairs of Fabric B and Fabric C for the wall quilt/*28 pairs for the queen*. Fabric C should be on the left as shown in Figure 4-13C.

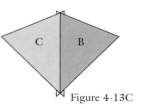

Figure 4-13C

4. Piece the 12 octagons for the wall quilt/ *16 for the queen,* using four C/C quarter-block units for each (Figure 4-14).

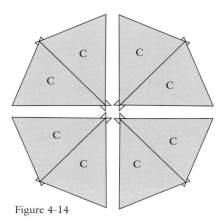

Figure 4-14

5. Add the appropriate corner triangles to make the C1 and C2 blocks, shown below. Press allowances toward the corner triangles. You need eight C1 blocks (Figure 4-15) for the wall quilt/ *12 for the queen,* and four C2 corner blocks (Figure 4-16) for either size.

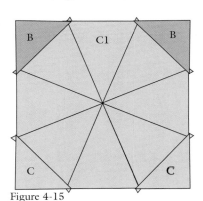

Figure 4-15

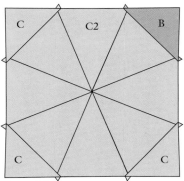

Figure 4-16

Arranging the Quilt and Piecing the B Blocks

1. Following the assembly diagram for the wall quilt (page 48) or queen quilt (page 51), arrange the A and C blocks on a flat surface, such as a design wall (page 15) leaving space between them for the B blocks.

2. You will use a set of four matching A/B quarter-block units around each A block, so that the kaleidoscope effect extends into the adjacent blocks. Working around one A block at a time, place identical units on the right, left, top, and bottom sides of each block. (Figure 4-17A shows the lower right corner.)

3. Following the assembly diagram, fill in around the A/B units with C/B and C/C units to complete the B1, B2, and B3 blocks (Figure 4-17B, page 48).

Figure 4-17A

Figure 4-17B

4. Piece blocks B1 (Figure 4-18A), B2 (Figure 4-18B) and B3 (Figure 4-18C). Work on one block at a time, using a flat surface to transfer the block to your sewing area.

5. As you piece each block, add the corner triangles as shown in Figures 4-19A–C. Press seam allowances toward the center of the block. This way, the seams will alternate when you sew the blocks together. Return each finished block to its position in the quilt, being careful not to rotate it.

Diamond Ring Wall Quilt Assembly

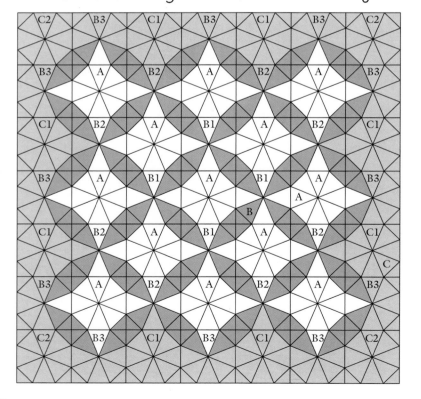

Color Key	
☐	Main Fabric A
▨	Ring Fabric B
▨	Border Fabric C

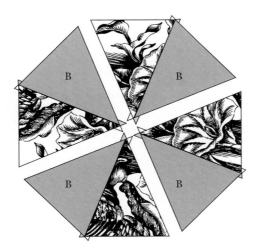

Figure 4-18A

Figure 4-19A

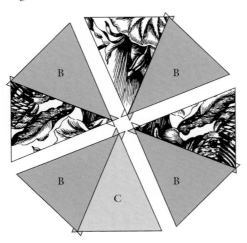

Figure 4-18B

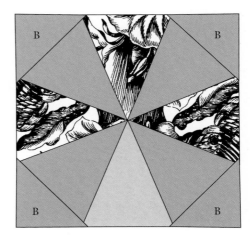

Figure 4-19B

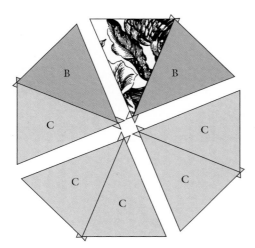

Figure 4-18C

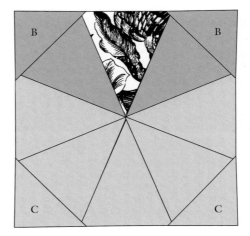

Figure 4-19C

Plate 42: 48 PARROT DIAMOND RING by author, 1997, 90" x 90". Careful fabric placement gives this design the illusion of "rings" without curved seams. (Pattern instructions begin on page 42.)

Assembling the Quilt

Pay close attention to the placement and orientation of each block. It's easy to get them mixed up. For easier handling, piece the queen blocks in nine-block units, as shown in the quilt assembly diagram.

Finishing the Quilt

See Chapter Eight for suggestions on quilting design and binding. Prepare the backing by piecing together two 1½-yard lengths of backing fabric for wall/*three 2¾-yard lengths for queen*. Layer, quilt, and bind.

Diamond Ring Queen Quilt Assembly

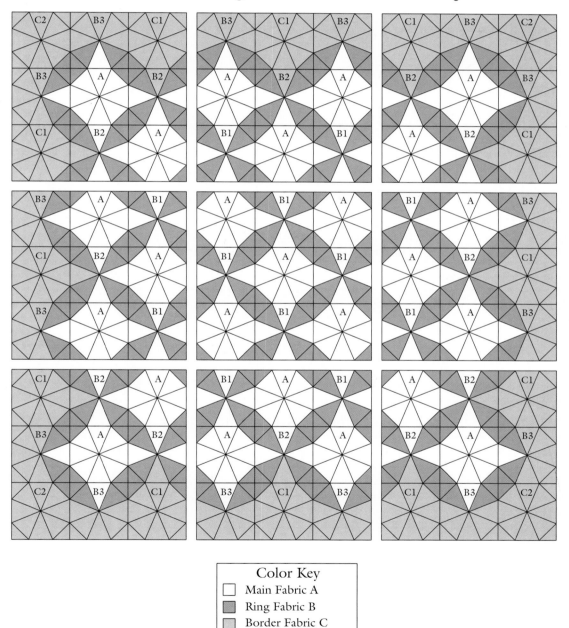

Color Key

☐ Main Fabric A
▨ Ring Fabric B
▨ Border Fabric C

Chapter Five

45° Diamond Magic

LeMoyne Star Baby or Wall Quilt

SAM'S MENAGERIE
See Plate 44, page 54   Finished Quilt: 40½" x 50"
Skill Level: Easy   Finished Block: 9½" (12 blocks)

LeMoyne Star Throw Quilt

ARABESQUE
See Plate 45, page 68   Finished Quilt: 55" x 70"
Skill Level: Intermediate   Finished Block: 12" (12 blocks)

Hands All Around Wall Quilt (begins on page 62)

Hybrid Lilies Wall Quilt (begins on page 64)

Fabric Requirements
(Measurements in yards unless otherwise indicated.)

If the design repeat of Main Fabric A is		6"–10"	11"–14"	15"–20"	21"–27"	over 27"
You will need this many yards	Baby or Wall*	2½	3½	5	6¾	8 repeats
	Throw	2½	3½	5	6¾	8 repeats
	Hands All Around Wall	leftovers from an 8-repeat stack				
	Hybrid Lilies Wall**	1½	2	2¾	3¾	4 repeats

Additional Fabrics	Baby or Wall	Throw	Hands All Around Wall	Hybrid Lilies Wall
Background Fabric B	1½	3¼	¾	3
Accent Fabric C	¼ narrow border	1 sashing	¼ leaves	1 narrow border, leaves, stems
Petal Fabric D			¼	
Backing	2¾	3½ piece crosswise	⅞	3⅝ piece lengthwise
Binding (cut 2½" strips crosswise)	½	½	¼	½

*Includes border 3.

**You will also need ½ yard of paper-backed fusing web for the appliqué and a 6" x 7" piece of plastic-coated freezer paper for the stem-placement guide.

Whacking 45° Diamonds

Plate 43

The diamond shape used for the LeMoyne Star and Hybrid Lily projects has two edges on the cross grain of the fabric and two on the bias.

Whacking Main Fabric Diamonds for the Block Kits

1. Refer to the Stack-n-Whack chart for your project to determine the size of the guide piece you will need. Using the basic stacking method, cut and stack eight identical repeats of Main Fabric A for all projects except the Hybrid Lilies, which has only four repeats.

2. Trim about ¼" from the pinned edge of the fabric stack, if necessary, to get a smooth edge. Cut a strip through all eight layers, using the width given in the Stack-n-Whack Chart. (Figure 5-1 shows a 3" strip being cut.)

3. Lay the ruler down on the strip set with the 45° line along one edge of the strips. Since the placement of this line varies on different brands of rulers, your ruler may be positioned differently from the one in Figure 5-2. Place the edge of the ruler far enough in

to avoid the selvages. Cut along the edge through all layers. Set aside this first cut. It is scrap fabric.

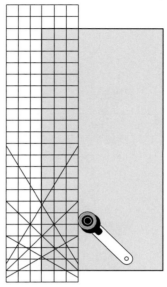

Figure 5-1

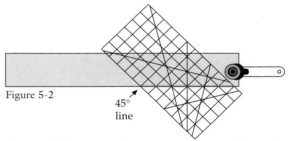

Figure 5-2   45° line

4. Carefully turn the strip set around so the angled edge is to your left (or to your right if you are left-handed). Lay the ruler down and measure over from the angled edge, using the same measurement you used in Step 2. Line up the vertical ruler line with the angled edge and the 45° line with one straight edge (Figure 5-3). Cut a 45° diamond. Each stack of diamonds is a block kit. You may want to check a diamond against the accuracy guide, page 105. Set these kits aside.

5. Repeat the process for the number of strip sets given in the Stack-n-Whack chart, removing the pins as you go to avoid damaging your blade. You should get at least four block kits

Plate 44: SAM'S MENAGERIE by author, 1996. A fun children's print and a simple setting make this a favorite for a quick gift. (Pattern instructions begin on page 52.)

from each strip set. Each star kit consists of eight identical repeats, enough for one star. Each Hybrid Lily kit consists of four identical repeats, enough for one lily flower.

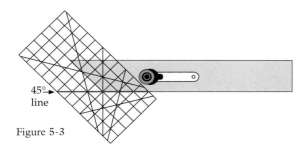

Figure 5-3

Whacking Accent Diamonds

These diamonds are not cut from identical repeats. Fold fabric in half lengthwise and cut the strip width according to the project directions. Unfold, stack the strips, and cut into diamonds following Steps 3 and 4. You do not need to pin these in sets, just stack them.

Piecing the LeMoyne Star Blocks

Piece 12 blocks for the baby or wall quilt and for the throw.

You can use the diamonds in each block kit with either tip in the center. You may want to lay out the pieces and preview the block both ways before sewing, because the results can be dramatically different (Figure 5-4A–B, page 57). Once you have decided which tip you would like in the center, *place a reference pin at that end* on each diamond in the block kit

Stack-n-Whack Chart for LeMoyne Star Baby or Wall Quilt			
Guide Piece...	**Stack...**	**Whack...**	**To Make...**
21" wide x one full repeat long	8 identical repeats of Main Fabric A	(3) 2½" x 21" strips	(12) 45° diamond block kits (4 per strip)
For fabrics with a repeat under 8", you will need a second stack; cut two strips from the first stack and one strip from the second.			

Stack-n-Whack Chart for LeMoyne Star Throw Quilt			
Guide Piece...	**Stack...**	**Whack...**	**To Make...**
21" wide x one full repeat long	8 identical repeats of Main Fabric A	(3) 3" x 21" strips	(12) 45° diamond block kits (4 per strip)
For fabrics with a repeat under 9", you will need a second stack; cut two strips from the first stack and one strip from the second.			

(Figure 5-5). The pin will remind you not to sew the x or y triangles to the sides adjacent to the center point. Follow the references pins in Figures 5-6A–5-10B to help you orient the pieces correctly.

1. Place the block kit next to your machine with the tips of the diamonds that will be the center (the tips with the reference pins) closest to you. Sew a background x triangle to the top right edge of the diamond (Figure 5-6A). The top corner of the triangle should line up with the tip of the diamond. The triangle will extend ¼" at its other end. Finger press the triangle open (Figure 5-6B). Repeat for three more diamonds. These are the left halves of the quarter-blocks.

2. Add background y triangles to the opposite sides of each of the four left halves (Figure 5-7A), lining up the lower edges of x and y. Press the seam allowances toward the background triangles. Take care not to stretch the bias edges (Figure 5-7B) as you work. You can now remove the reference pins from these four units.

3. Turn the remaining four diamonds so that the pins are at the top. Take a diamond from this set and sew an x triangle to the lower right edge of the diamond (Figure 5-8A). Note the position of the reference pin. Finger press the triangle open. Repeat for three more diamonds (Figure 5-8B). These are the right halves of the quarter-blocks.

Cutting Main Fabric A

Follow the directions for whacking 45° Diamonds on page 54.

Cutting Background Fabric B – Baby or Wall Quilt

Fabric and Position	First Cut	Second Cut	Third Cut
Background Fabric B x triangles	(4) 2⅞" strips across width	(48) 2⅞" squares	Cut once on the diagonal to make 96 half-square triangles
Background Fabric B y triangles	(5) 3¾" strips across width	(48) 3¾" squares	Cut once on the diagonal to make 96 half-square triangles

Cutting Background Fabric B – Throw Quilt

Fabric and Position	First Cut	Second Cut	Third Cut
Background Fabric B x triangles	(4) 3⅜" strips across width	(48) 3⅜" squares	Cut once on the diagonal to make 96 half-square triangles
Background Fabric B y triangles	(6) 4⅜" strips across width	(48) 4⅜" squares	Cut once on the diagonal to make 96 half-square triangles

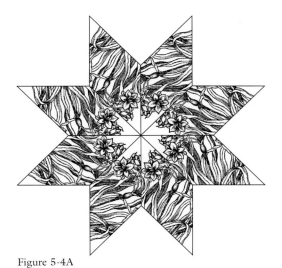

Figure 5-4A

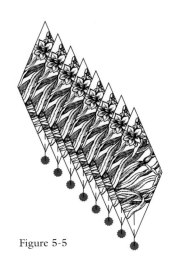

Figure 5-4B

Figure 5-5

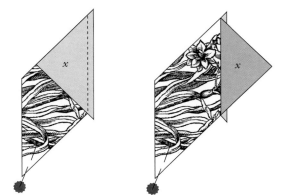

Figures 5-6A–B: Stop! Sew only four diamonds.

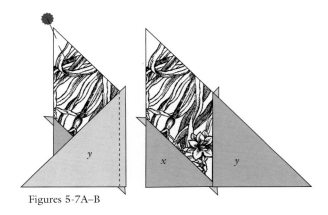

Figures 5-7A–B

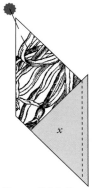

Figures 5-8A–B

4. Take the four right halves and add background y triangles as shown (Figure 5-9A). Press the seam allowances toward the background triangles. Remove the reference pins from these four units (Figure 5-9B).

5. Position a left half and a right half as shown (Figure 5-10A). Sew the two halves together, matching the triangle tips and the seams of the diamonds (Figure 5-10B). Clip

the triangle tips along the just-sewn seam. Repeat with the other three sets. Carefully press the allowances open (Figure 5-10C).

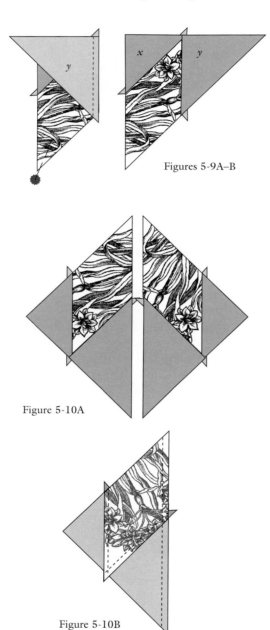

Figures 5-9A–B

Figure 5-10A

Figure 5-10B

6. Sew the quarter-blocks together in pairs, matching the triangle tips and the crossed seams at the center. Clip the triangle tips along the seams. Press allowances open.

7. Sew the half-blocks together, clip the tips, and press the allowances open to complete the block (Figure 5-11).

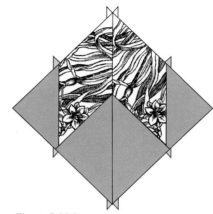

Figure 5-10C

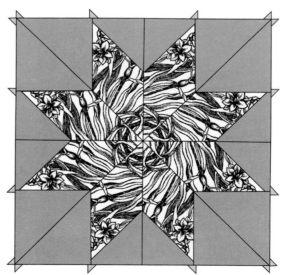

Figure 5-11

Assembling the Baby or Wall Quilt

Following the quilt assembly diagram on page 59, pin the blocks to a design wall or lay them out on the floor to decide on the block placement. Sew the vertical seams in each row, then sew the horizontal rows together.

Adding Borders – Baby or Wall Quilt	
Fabric and Position	**Cut**
Background Fabric B – Border 1	(4) 2½" strips across width
Accent Fabric C – Border 2	(5) 1½" strips across width
Main Fabric A – Border 3	(4) 3½" strips x 45", cut lengthwise or (5) 3½" strips across width

1. For these butted borders, measure the length down the center of the quilt and trim two strips of Background Fabric B to this length. Pin and sew the borders to the quilt.

2. Measure the width across the center of the quilt, including side borders, and trim the other two strips of Background Fabric B to this length. Pin and sew these borders.

3. Add the borders of Accent Fabric C and Main Fabric A in the same manner. If you cut strips across the width for border 3, piece together 1½ strips for each side and use the two remaining strips for the top and bottom.

LeMoyne Star Baby or Wall Quilt Assembly

Cutting the Sashing, Cornerstones, and Borders – Throw Quilt	
Fabric and Position	**Cut**
Background Fabric B – Border	(4) 4" strips x 70" cut parallel to selvages
Background Fabric B – Sashing and Cornerstones	(17) 1½" strips x 70" cut parallel to selvages
Accent Fabric C – Sashing and Cornerstones	(20) 1½" strips x 34" to 36" cut parallel to selvages

Piecing the Sashing and Cornerstones

1. Piece the Accent Fabric C strips together in pairs, end to end, to make 10 strips that are 67" to 70" long.

2. Piece eight strip sets of B-C-B, as shown in diagram (a), for sashing and cornerstone assembly on page 61. Press the allowances toward the center of the strip. Cut the sets into 12½" long sections or the average measurement of your blocks if they are consistently larger or smaller than 12½". Trim out the sections where you pieced the accent fabric strips end to end in Step 1. You will need 31 sections for the sashing as shown in diagram (b). Reserve the rest for the cornerstones.

3. Piece one set of C-B-C, see diagram (c). Press the allowances away from the center of the strip.

4. Cut the C-B-C set and the remainder of the B-C-B sets crosswise into 1½" lengths for the cornerstones. You will need 20 B-C-B pieces and 40 C-B-C pieces.

5. Sew these pieces into 20 Nine-Patch cornerstones, see diagram (d). Press allowances away from the center. The accent fabric should be in the center and the four corners.

Assembling the Quilt

1. Pin the blocks to a design wall or lay them out on the floor to decide on the arrangement. Lay the sashing strips between each block and around the outer edge of each block as shown in the quilt assembly diagram on page 61. Place the cornerstones at each intersection.

2. Sew the vertical seams in each row, then sew the horizontal rows together.

3. Measure the length down the center of the quilt and cut two side borders this length from the reserved 4" strips of Background Fabric B. Pin and sew these borders.

4. Measure the width across the center of the quilt, including side borders, and cut the remaining two border strips to fit. Pin and sew these borders.

Finishing the Quilt

See Chapter Eight for suggestions on quilting design and binding. Prepare the backing by piecing together two 1¾-yard lengths of backing fabric. Layer, quilt, and bind.

LeMoyne Star Throw Quilt
Sashing and Cornerstone Assembly

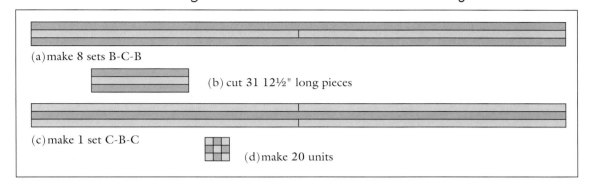

(a) make 8 sets B-C-B

(b) cut 31 12½" long pieces

(c) make 1 set C-B-C

(d) make 20 units

LeMoyne Star
Throw Quilt Assembly

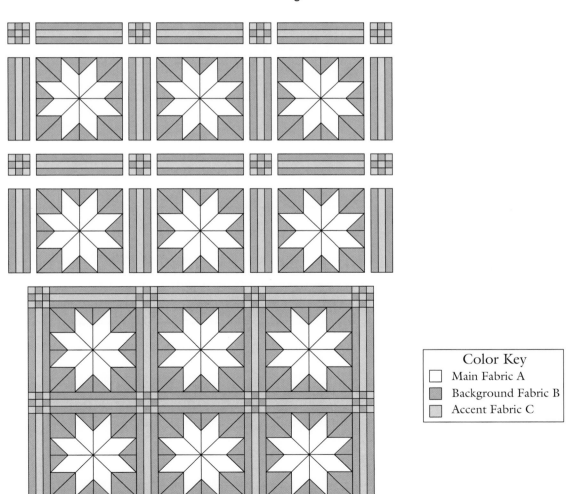

Color Key
☐ Main Fabric A
■ Background Fabric B
■ Accent Fabric C

Hands All Around Wall Quilt

HANDS ALL AROUND
See Plate 13A & 13B, page 13   Finished Quilt: 26" x 26"
Skill Level: Easy   Finished Block: 24" (1 block)

Cutting Main Fabric A

See page 52 for yardage. Follow the directions for whacking 45° diamonds on page 53.

Stack-n-Whack Chart for Hands All Around Quilt			
Guide Piece...	**Stack...**	**Whack...**	**To Make...**
8½" wide x 3½" long	8 identical repeats of Main Fabric A	(1) 3" x 8" strips	(1) 45° diamond block kit
You may be able to use leftover stacked repeats (eg., from a Pinwheel quilt) for this project.			

Cutting Fabrics B, C, and D – Hands All Around Quilt			
Fabric and Position	**First Cut**	**Second Cut**	**Third Cut**
Background Fabric B Border	(4) 1½" strips across width		
Background Fabric B *x* triangles	(2) 3⅜" strips across width	(16) 3⅜" squares	Cut once on the diagonal to make 32 half-square triangles
Background Fabric B *y* triangles	(2) 4⅜" strips across width	(16) 4⅜" squares	Cut once on the diagonal to make 32 half-square triangles
Leaf Fabric C	(1) 3" strip across width	(8) 3" 45° diamonds	
Petal Fabric D	(2) 3" strips across width	(16) 3" 45° diamonds	

Piecing the Hands All Around Block and Adding the Border

Piece one LeMoyne Star block, following the instructions beginning on page 55. Piece quarter-blocks from the leaf and petal fabrics as shown in the quilt assembly diagram. Arrange and sew the quarter-blocks as shown to make one Hands All Around block. Sew one border strip to each side, trimming the extra length.

Finishing the Quilt

See Chapter Eight for suggestions on quilting design and binding. Layer, quilt, and bind.

Hands All Around Wall Quilt Assembly

Use these units...

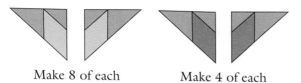

Make 8 of each   Make 4 of each

Color Key
☐ Main Fabric A
■ Leaf Fabric
■ Petal Fabric

to make these quarter-blocks.

Make 4   Make 4   Make 4

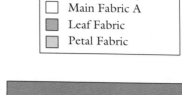

Hybrid Lilies
Wall Quilt Assembly

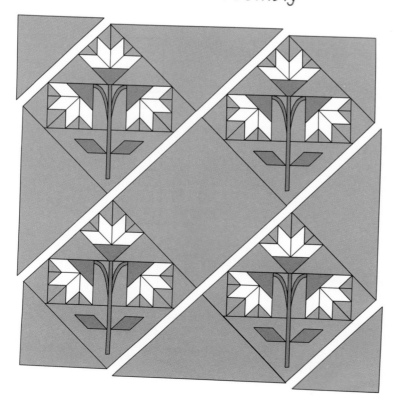

Color Key
☐ Main Fabric A
■ Background Fabric B
■ Accent Fabric C

Hybrid Lilies Wall Quilt

HYBRID LILIES
See Plate 46, page 68
Skill Level: Advanced Intermediate

Finished Quilt: 58" x 58"
Finished Block: 18½" (4 blocks)

Cutting Main Fabric A

See page 52 for yardage. Follow the directions for whacking 45° diamonds on page 53.

Stack-n-Whack Chart for Hybrid Lilies Wall Quilt

Guide Piece...	Stack...	Whack...	To Make...
21" wide x one full repeat long	4 identical repeats of Main Fabric A	(3) 2½" x 21" strips	(12) 45° diamond block kits (4 per strip)

For fabrics with a repeat under 8", you will need a second stack; cut two strips from the first stack and one strip from the second.

Cutting Background Fabric B – Hybrid Lilies
Cut the Fabric B pieces in the order given below and label them for easier piecing.

Position in Quilt (block diagram, page 69)	First Cut	Second Cut	Third Cut
Setting Triangles Sides of Quilt	(1) 28" strip across width	(1) 28" square	Cut twice diagonally to make 4 side triangles
Hybrid Lily Block *q* triangles	(2) 7¼" strips cut from remainder of 27½" strip above	(4) 7¼" squares	Cut once diagonally for 8 half-square triangles
Setting Triangles Corners of Quilt	(1) 14" strip across width	(2) 14" squares	Cut once diagonally for 4 half-square triangles
Square Center of Quilt	(1) 19" strip across width	(1) 19" square	
Hybrid Lily Block triangles	(2) 6⅛" strips cut from the remainder of 19" strip above	(4) 6⅛" squares	Cut once diagonally for 8 half-square triangles
rid Lily Block gles	(1) 14⅞" strip across width	(2) 14⅞" squares	Cut once diagonally for 4 half-square triangles
Lily Block les	(2) 7⅜" strips cut from remainder of 14⅞" strip above	(4) 7⅜" x 5½" rectangles	
	(2) 2⅞" strips across width	(24) 2⅞" squares	Cut once diagonally for 48 half-square triangles
	(2) 3¾" strips across width	(12) 3¾" squares	Cut once diagonally for 24 half-square triangles

Cutting Accent Fabric C – Hybrid Lilies			
Position in Quilt	**First Cut**	**Second Cut**	**Third Cut**
Border	(6) 1" strips across width		
Lily Flower Bases z triangles	(1) 4⅞" strip across width	(6) 4⅞" squares	Cut once on the diagonal to make 12 half-square triangles
For the leaves and stems, fuse a 14" square of paper-backed fusing web to the wrong side of a square of Fabric C. Trim the fabric even with the edges of the paper.			

Piecing the Lily Flower Units

Each of the four Hybrid Lily blocks has three lily flower units and an appliquéd stem and leaf section. Piece all the lily flower units first so that you can choose which three to use for each block. To avoid confusion, piece one unit at a time, at least through Step 6.

You can use the diamonds in each block kit with either tip toward the center of the block. You may want to lay out the pieces and preview the block each way before sewing, because the results can be dramatically different (Figures 5-12A–B). Once you have decided which end you would like in the center, place a reference pin at that end on each diamond in the block kit (Figure 5-13). The pin will remind you not to sew triangles to the sides adjacent to the center point. Follow the reference pins in Figures 5-14A–5-17A to orient the pieces correctly.

Figures 5-12A–B

1. Place a block kit next to the machine with the pin end closest to you. Sew an x triangle to the top right edge of one diamond (Figure 5-14A). The triangle's top corner should line up with the diamond tip; the triangle will extend ¼" at the other end. Finger press the triangle open (Figure 5-14B). Repeat for one more diamond.

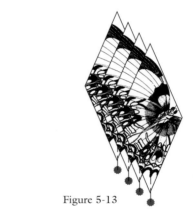

Figure 5-13

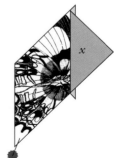

Figures 5-14A–B

2. Take one of the diamonds from Step 1 and add a background y triangle to the opposite side (Figure 5-15A), lining up the lower edges of x and y. Press the allowance toward

the background, taking care not to stretch the bias edges (Figure 5-15B). Do not add anything to the other diamond from this pair. You can now remove the reference pins from these two units.

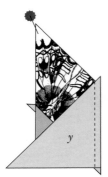

Figures 5-15A–B

3. Turn the two remaining diamonds so that the pins are at the top. Take a diamond from this set and sew an *x* triangle to the lower right edge of the diamond (Figure 5-16A). Finger press the triangle open (Figure 5-16B). Repeat for the last diamond in the kit.

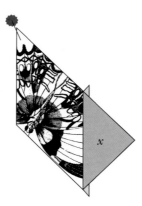

Figures 5-16A–B

4. Take one of the diamonds from Step 3 and add a background *y* triangle as shown in Figure 5-17A. Press allowance toward the background (Figure 5-17B). Do not add anything to the remaining diamond. Remove the reference pins from these two units.

5. Place two units side by side to see how they are joined (Figure 5-18A). Sew the two triangle units together, matching the triangle

tips and the seams of the diamonds (Figure 5-18B). Clip the triangle tips along the seam. Press allowances open (Figure 5-18C).

Figures 5-17A–B

Figures 5-18A–C

6. Add the other two diamond/triangle units from Step 4 to the left and right sides of this unit (Figures 5-19 and 5-20). Clip the triangle tips along the seams. Press allowances open.

7. To add the *z* flower base triangle, center the corner of the triangle on the diagonal

seam line of the petal unit and pin in place. Turn the unit over and stitch with the base on the bottom so that you can see where the seams of the petal pieces cross. Press allowances toward the base (Figure 5-21). Make 12 of these units.

Figure 5-19

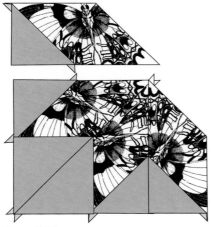

Figure 5-20

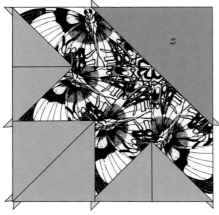

Figure 5-21

Adding the Stems and Leaves

1. Fold the *s* triangle and the *t* rectangle in half and press lightly to mark the center line, shown by the dotted line in Figure 5-22. Sew *s* to *t*, matching the center points and leaving about 1" open at each end of the seam (partial seam).

2. Remove the paper backing from the fused square of Fabric C and cut the square in half on the diagonal. From one half, cut ½" strips along the bias edge for the stems. Set aside the four longest strips for the center stems of the four blocks. From the other half, cut 2"-wide strips. Cut eight 45° diamonds from the strips for the leaves (Figure 5-23).

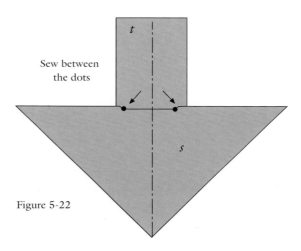

Sew between the dots

Figure 5-22

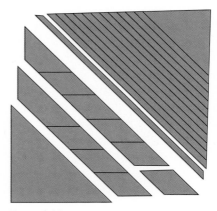

Figure 5-23

Plate 45: ARABESQUE by author, 1996. A dozen star blocks are placed in a classic setting with sashing and Nine-Patch cornerstones. (LeMoyne Star throw quilt directions begin on page 52.)

Plate 46: HYBRID LILIES by author, 1996. Three unique flowers bloom on each lily plant—a gardener's dream! This simplified version of the traditional Carolina Lily block has machine appliquéd stems and leaves. (Hybrid Lilies wall quilt directions begin on page 64.)

3. Trace the Stem Placement Guides on page 106 onto freezer paper and cut them out. With the shiny side of the freezer paper facing the right side of the fabric, press the guides to the *t* rectangle. Use a dry iron and light pressure.

4. Lay short strips of the ½" bias-cut Fabric C along the curved lines, using the tip of the iron to ease the strips in place. The top ends of the strips should extend just past the edges of the rectangle. Trim the bottom ends of the strips at an angle so that they will be covered by the center stem (Plate 47).

Plate 47: Place the short stems next to the freezer-paper guides and press lightly. Cut stem at an angle.

5. Cut the center stem strip to 14½". Lay it in place on the pressed center line of the *s/t* unit. Press lightly.

6. Peel away the freezer paper and press the stems in place securely, following the fusing-web manufacturer's recommendations.

7. Place the diamond leaves with their top edges at 1¾" below the seam line (2" below the cut edge of triangle *s*), with the tips of the diamonds touching the stem and the edges parallel to the seam (Plate 48). Fuse in place.

8. Machine appliqué the stems and leaves, using a zigzag, blind-hem, or blanket stitch.

Use matching or invisible thread for a hand appliquéd effect or use a decorative thread, if you prefer. If you are not familiar with the appliqué settings for your sewing machine, check the owner's manual or consult your machine dealer for recommended stitches and setup. Do a test on scraps to find the settings you like best for width, length, and tension. If the stitch puckers, try using a tear-away stabilizer under the block.

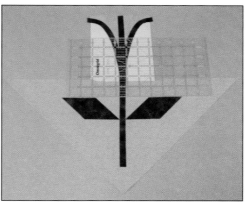

Plate 48: Use a ruler to place the leaves.

Piecing the Hybrid Lily Block

Decide which three flower units to use together for the blocks. Following the block diagram (Figure 5-24), place the lily flower units, *s/t* unit and background pieces *q* and *r* as they will appear in the finished block.

Figure 5-24

1. Sew the *q* triangles to the left and right edges of the top flower (Figure 5-25A). The triangle tips will not cross at the flower base. Press the allowances toward the background (Figure 5-25B). Lay a ruler along the bias edges of the *q* triangles and trim off the tip of the flower base (Figure 5-25C). (This assembly method gives room for the stem to meet the base, so the top flower will not look as if someone tried to snip it off.)

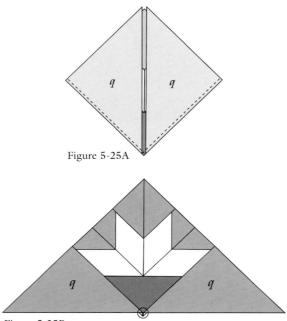

Figure 5-25A

Figure 5-25B

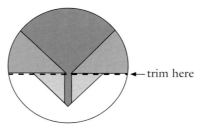

←— trim here

Figure 5-25C

2. Sew the *r* triangles to the left and right flower units (Figure 5-26). The *r* triangle tips will extend past the flower units at the lower edge. Press the seam allowances toward the background. Trim the excess from the *r* triangles (Figure 5-27).

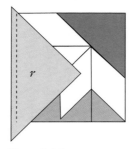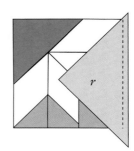

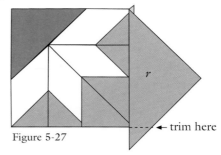

Figure 5-26

←— trim here

Figure 5-27

3. Sew the left and right flower units to the *t* rectangle. Press allowances toward the flowers. Complete the partial seam between the *s* triangles and the flower units. Press allowances toward the *s* triangle. Add the top flower unit and press allowances toward the top.

4. If the pieced block measures more than 19" including the seam allowance, trim it evenly along the two lower sides to measure exactly 19".

Assembling the Quilt

If you plan to add machine trapunto, see Chapter Eight (page 95). You may want to baste the batting for the trapunto in place before sewing the blocks together.

Referring to the quilt assembly diagram on page 63, pin the blocks to a design wall or lay them out on the floor to decide on the block placement. Sew the blocks and side triangles together in diagonal rows, being careful not to stretch the bias edges. Sew the diagonal rows together and add the corner triangles. Trim any excess fabric from the side and corner triangles.

Adding the Borders

1. Piece together the six strips of Fabric C to make one long strip. Measure the length down the center of the quilt and cut two border strips this length. Pin and sew these borders.

2. Measure the width across the center of the quilt, including the side borders, and cut two strips this length. Pin and sew these to the top and bottom.

3. From the remaining Main Fabric A, cut four lengthwise strips, 3" x 59", or piece together six crosswise strips 3" wide. Measure the length down the center of the quilt and cut two border strips this length. Pin and sew these borders. Repeat for the top and bottom borders.

Finishing the Quilt

See Chapter eight for suggestions on quilting design and binding. Prepare the backing by piecing together two 1¾-yard lengths of the backing fabric. Use your favorite methods for layering, quilting, and binding.

Chapter Six

60° Triangle Magic

Plate 49: SUMMER BOUQUETS by author, 1997. The photographs in Chapter Two show this quilt in progress.

Hexagon Star Throw Quilt

SUMMER BOUQUETS
See Plate 49, page 72   Finished Quilt: 56" x 63"
Skill Level: Easy   Finished Block: 8½" x 9¾" (18 blocks)

Hexagon Star Wall Quilt

HOFFMAN CHALLENGE
See Plate 50, page 81   Finished Quilt: 35½" x 37"
Skill Level: Intermediate   Finished Block: 5½" x 6¼" (18 blocks)

Hexagon Star Double Quilt

STARFISH AND SEA URCHINS
See Plate 51, page 81   Finished Quilt: 78" x 102""
Skill Level: Intermediate   Finished Block: 8½" x 9¾" (32 blocks)

Fabric Requirements
(Measurements in yards unless otherwise indicated.)

If the design repeat of Main Fabric A is		6"–10"	11"–14"	15"–20"	21"–27"	over 27"
You will need this many yards	Throw*	4	5¼	5¼	5¼	6 repeats
	Wall*	2	2¾	4	5¼	6 repeats
	Double**	5¼	6	6	6½	6 repeats

Additional Fabrics	Throw	Wall	Double
Background Fabric B	1¼	⅝	2½
Accent Fabric C	1 star points & border	½ star points	3¼ star points & border
Backing	3½ piece crosswise	1¼	6 piece lengthwise
Binding (cut 2½" strips crosswise)	⅝	⅜	¾

*Includes one border.
**Includes triangles for pieced border.

Whacking 60° Triangles

This triangle has three equal sides and a 60° angle at each point. By cutting diamonds first, then cutting the diamonds in half, you will get accurate triangles without having to flip the ruler back and forth.

Whacking Main Fabric Triangles for the Block Kits

1. Refer to the Stack-n-Whack chart for your project to determine the size of the guide piece needed. Using the basic stacking method, cut and stack six identical repeats of Main Fabric A.

2. Trim about ¼" from the pinned edge of the fabric stack, if necessary, to get a smooth edge. Cut a strip through all six layers, using the width given in the Stack-n-Whack chart. (Figure 6-1 shows how to cut a 5" strip.)

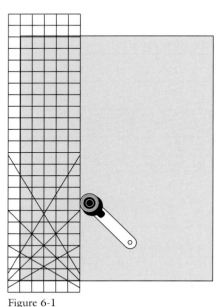

Figure 6-1

3. Lay the ruler down on the strip set with the 60° line along one edge. Since the placement of this line varies on different brands of rulers, your ruler may be positioned differently from the ones in the illustration (Figures 6-2A and B). Place the edge of the ruler far enough in to avoid the selvages. Cut through all the layers, and set aside this first cut. This is scrap fabric.

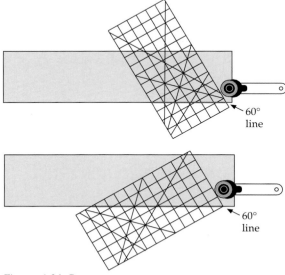

Figures 6-2A–B

> **NOTE**
> Some rulers have a 30° line, which corresponds to the 60° line on other brands. If the ruler has 30° and 60° lines, use the 60° line. You can also use an equilateral triangle ruler for Step 3 and switch to a rectangular ruler for the rest of the cutting.

4. Carefully turn the strip set around so the angled edge is to your left (or to your right if you are left-handed). Lay the ruler down and measure over from the angled edge, using the same measurement you used in Step 2. Line up the vertical ruler line with the angled edge and the 60° line with one straight edge (Figure 6-3). Cut the diamond.

5. Cut the diamond in half (Figure 6-4). You now have two block kits. Pin through each kit on the straight-grain edge (the original edge of the strip) to help you keep the pieces together and remind you which way to sew

them (Figure 6-5). Check the triangles against the accuracy guide in the Appendix, page 108. Set these kits aside. Continue cutting block kits from the strip. You may be able to get an extra block kit at the end of the strip by cutting a partial diamond (Figure 6-6).

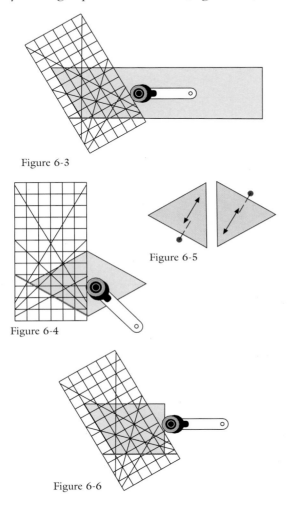

Figure 6-3

Figure 6-4

Figure 6-5

Figure 6-6

6. Repeat the process for the number of strip sets given in the project directions, using a second stack if necessary. Remove the pins in the stack as you go.

Whacking Border, Background, and Accent Triangles

These triangles are not cut from identical repeats. For the B and C triangles, fold the fabric in half lengthwise and cut the strip width according to the project directions. Unfold, stack the strips, and cut into triangles, following Steps 3 though 5. You do not need to pin these in sets but try to keep them stacked with all the straight-grain edges on one side.

Some of the Fabric A triangles used in the border of the Hexagon Star double quilt can be cut from stacked repeats left over from cutting the block kits, or you may prefer to save the stacks for another project. Although these triangles will be in matching sets, you will probably want to mix them up and use them randomly in the border units. Cut additional strips of Fabric A, if necessary, to get enough triangles.

Whacking Half-Triangles

To create straight-sided edges, you will add half-triangles to the center setting units of the throw or wall quilt, or to the border units of the double quilt. These half-triangles are cut from slightly larger 60° triangles, which are cut through the center along the straight grain (Figure 6-7). Each triangle will yield two half-triangles (Figure 6-8). Keep the left halves and right halves stacked separately until you are ready to piece the setting or border units.

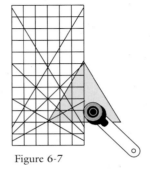

Figure 6-7 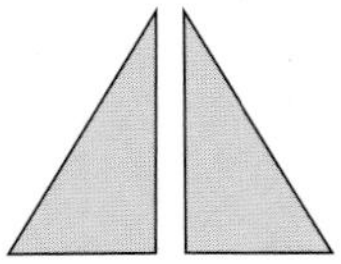   Figure 6-8

Cutting Main Fabric A

Follow the directions for whacking 60° Triangles on page 74.
Hexagon Star Double Quilt directions begin on page 80.

Stack-n-Whack Chart for Hexagon Star Throw Quilt

Guide Piece...	Stack...	Whack...	To Make...
21" wide x one full repeat long*	6 identical repeats of Main Fabric A	(3) 5" x 21" strips	(18) 60° triangle block kits (6 per strip)

*For fabrics with a repeat under 8", use three full repeats for the length of the guide piece. For fabrics with a repeat of 8" to 15", use two full repeats for the length of the guide piece.

Stack-n-Whack Chart for Hexagon Star Wall Quilt

Guide Piece...	Stack...	Whack...	To Make...
16" wide x one full repeat long*	6 identical repeats of Main Fabric A	(3) 3½" x 16" strips	(18) 60° triangle block kits (6 per strip)

For fabrics with a repeat of 7" to 11", you will need a second stack; cut two strips from the first stack and one from the second.
*For fabrics with a repeat under 7", use two full repeats for the length of the guide piece.

Stack-n-Whack Chart for Hexagon Star Double Quilt

Guide Piece...	Stack...	Whack...	To Make...
21" wide x one full repeat long*	6 identical repeats of Main Fabric A	(6) 5" x 21" strips	(32) 60° triangle block kits (6 per strip)

You will need two stacks; cut three strips from each stack.
*For fabrics with a repeat under 8", use three full repeats for the length of the guide piece. For fabrics with a repeat of 8" to 15", use two full repeats for the length of the guide piece.

Cutting Accent Fabric C (Star Points) – Throw and Wall Quilts

	First Cut	Second Cut
Throw	(5) 5" strips across width	(54) 60° triangles (12 per strip)
Wall	(3) 3½" strips across width	(54) 60° triangles (18 per strip)

Cutting Background Fabric B – Throw Quilt

Position in Quilt	First Cut	Second Cut	Third Cut
Center Setting Triangles	(4) 5" strips across width	(42) 60° triangles (12 per strip)	
Center Setting Half-Triangles	(1) 5⅜" strips across width	(12) 60° triangles	Cut up the center on the straight grain to make (24) half-triangles

Cutting Background Fabric B – Wall Quilt

Position in Quilt	First Cut	Second Cut	Third Cut
Center Setting Triangles	(3) 3½" strips across width	(42) 60° triangles (18 per strip)	
Center Setting Half-Triangles	(1) 3⅞" strips across width	(12) 60° triangles	Cut up the center on the straight grain to make (24) half-triangles

Piecing the Hexagon Star Blocks

Piece 18 hexagon blocks, following the illustrated instructions below. Add the star points to the hexagon blocks, following the instructions on page 78. If you have not yet chosen your background fabric, lay some of the hexagon star blocks on various fabrics and select one.

1. Unpin one block kit (six identical triangles), taking note of the straight-grain edge. This will be the outside edge of the hexagon, and the opposite point will be the center. To keep from unintentionally turning a triangle, put a reference pin in each of the six triangles on that edge (Figure 6-9).

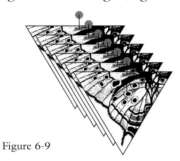

Figure 6-9

2. Making sure the pins are at the top, place the block kit next to your machine. Pick up the first two triangles and sew them, right sides together, along the right edge as shown in Figure 6-10. Repeat with the second pair of triangles. Press the seam allowances open.

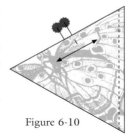

Figure 6-10

3. Take one of the remaining triangles and lay it to the right of one of the open pairs (Figure 6-11). Flip it over onto the pair and sew from the outer edge to the center. Repeat with the other pair and the last triangle. Clip the triangle tips that extend past the seam allowances. Press allowances open. You should have two identical halves (Figure 6-12, page 78). Remove the pins.

4. Place the halves right sides together and stitch across the center of the block, matching the crossed seams at the center. Press allowances open (Figure 6-13, page 78).

5. Piece all the hexagons. If you have not chosen a star-point fabric yet, do this now and cut the star-point triangles.

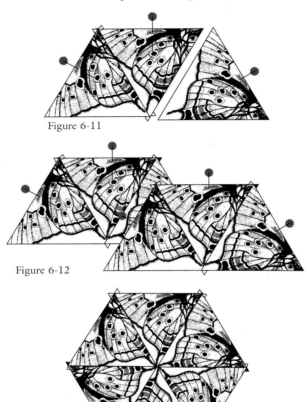

Figure 6-11

Figure 6-12

Figure 6-13

Adding the Star Points

1. Lay a star block next to your machine, right side up, with the center seam running vertically. Lay a star point on the center triangle, right sides together, with the straight-grain edge placed as shown by the arrow (Figure 6-14). The corners of the triangle should match up with the triangle tips that extend outside the star block. Sew this seam.

2. Continue to add one point to each block in this manner. Turn the blocks around and add a triangle to the opposite side to make a diamond-shaped block (Figure 6-15). Press allowances toward the star points. Take care not to stretch the bias edges.

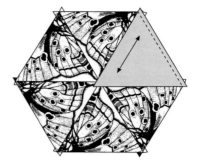

Figure 6-14

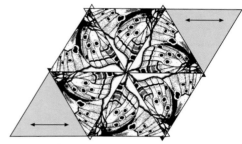

Figure 6-15

Adding the Half-Triangles

When you are assembling the Hexagon Star and the Morning Star quilts, you will need to add half-triangles to the 60° triangles at the ends of some of the rows. Figures 6-16 A–B show the fabric positions for the right half-triangles, and Figures 6-17A–B show the positions for the left half-triangles.

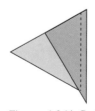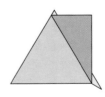

Figures 6-16A–B: (16A) Sewing position, (16B) finished unit.

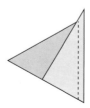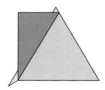

Figures 6-17A–B: (17A) Sewing position, (17B) finished unit.

Assembling the Hexagon Star Quilts

For the throw and wall sizes, piece the center setting units from Fabrics B and C, referring to the unit assembly diagram, page 82, and adding the half-triangles, described on page 78. Lay out the quilt according to the quilt assembly diagram, page 82. Sew the blocks together in horizontal rows, then sew the rows together.

Adding Borders – Throw Quilt	
Fabric and Position	**Cut**
Background Fabric B – Border 1	(5) 2½" strips across width
Accent Fabric C – Border 2	(6) 1½" strips across width
Main Fabric A – Border 3	(4) 3½" strips x 59" lengthwise strips

1. The borders for the throw quilt have butted corners. Piece together the five border 1 strips, end to end, to make one long strip. Measure the quilt top down the center and cut two strips this length. Sew the border strips to the long sides. Measure across the width, including the first border, and cut two strips this length. Sew these to the top and bottom.

2. Repeat for border 2.

3. Measure down the center of the quilt, including the first two borders, and cut two Fabric A border strips to this length. Sew these to the long sides. Measure across the width, including the third border, and cut the two remaining strips to this length. Sew these to the top and bottom.

Adding Borders – Wall Quilt	
Fabric and Position	**Cut**
Background Fabric B – Border 1	(4) 1" strips across width
Main Fabric A – Border 2	(4) 3½" strips x 35" lengthwise strips

1. For the butted borders for the wall size, measure the quilt top down the center and cut two border 1 strips this length. Sew the borders to the long sides. Measure across the width, including the first border, and cut two strips this length. Sew these to the top and bottom.

2. Repeat for border 2.

Cutting Accent Fabric C – Star Points and Border Triangles – Double Quilt			
Position in Quilt	**First Cut**	**Second Cut**	**Third Cut**
Block Star Points and Border Triangles	(19) 5" strips across width	(224) 60° triangles (12 per strip)	
Border Half-Triangles	(1) 5⅜" strips across width	(12) 60° triangles	Cut up the center on the straight grain to make (24) half-triangles

For the double quilt, add the star points to the hexagon blocks, following the illustrated instructions on page 78.

Cutting Main Fabric A and Background Fabric B Border Triangles – Double Quilt			
Fabric and Position	**First Cut**	**Second Cut**	**Third Cut**
Main Fabric A Border Triangles	(28) 5" half-width strips (cut from leftover stacks or remaining yardage)	(136) 60° triangles (5 per half-width strip)	
Main Fabric A Border Half-Triangles	(1) 5⅜" strip across width	(12) 60° triangles	Cut up the center on the straight grain to make (24) half-triangles
Background Fabric B Center Setting Triangles	(16) 5" strip across width	(192) 60° triangles (12 per strip)	

Piecing the Border Units for the Double

Following the border unit diagrams, page 82, piece Units B through I and the top and bottom quilt rows from Fabrics A, B and C. To add the half-triangles, refer to the illustrated instructions on page 78.

Finishing the Quilt – All sizes

See Chapter Eight for suggestions on quilting design and binding. Prepare the backing by piecing together two 1¾-yard lengths of backing fabric for the throw/*two 3-yard lengths for the double*. The wall quilt backing does not need to be pieced.

Plate 50: HOFFMAN CHALLENGE by author, 1995. Using the same fabric for the star points and background gives the Hexagon Star design a different look. (Hexagon Star wall quilt directions begin on page 73.)

Plate 51: STARFISH AND SEA URCHINS by author, 1997. An integrated pieced border complements a great collection of kaleidoscope blocks. (Hexagon Star double quilt directions begin on page 73.)

 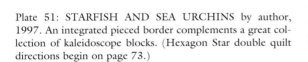

Hexagon Star
Throw or Wall Quilt Assembly

Hexagon Star
Throw or Wall Quilt
Center Setting Units

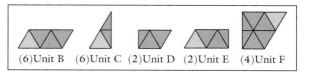

(6)Unit B (6)Unit C (2)Unit D (2)Unit E (4)Unit F

Hexagon Star Double Quilt Border Units

First, make hexagons B–G and half-hexagons H and I. Then, add the appropriate triangles to make the following units.

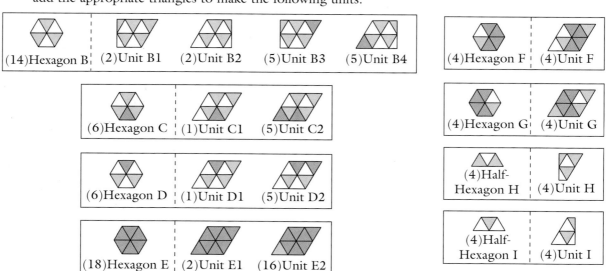

(14)Hexagon B | (2)Unit B1 | (2)Unit B2 | (5)Unit B3 | (5)Unit B4

(4)Hexagon F | (4)Unit F

(6)Hexagon C | (1)Unit C1 | (5)Unit C2

(4)Hexagon G | (4)Unit G

(6)Hexagon D | (1)Unit D1 | (5)Unit D2

(4)Half-Hexagon H | (4)Unit H

(18)Hexagon E | (2)Unit E1 | (16)Unit E2

(4)Half-Hexagon I | (4)Unit I

Hexagon Star Double Quilt Assembly

Color Key
- ☐ Main Fabric A
- ▨ Background Fabric B
- ▨ Accent Fabric C

Chapter Seven
60° Diamond Magic

Plate 52: IT'S NOT THE LATITUDE, IT'S THE ATTITUDE by author, 1997. Our Maine winters are long. Sometimes we have to quilt a tropical vacation! (Morning Star queen quilt directions begin on facing page.)

Morning Star Queen Quilt

IT'S NOT THE LATITUDE, IT'S THE ATTITUDE
See Plate 52, page 84
Skill Level: Advanced Intermediate
Finished Quilt: 96" x 105"
Finished Block: approx. 12" x 14" (39 star blocks)

Morning Star Wall Quilt

CHRISTMAS MORNING STAR
See Plate 53, page 92
Skill Level: Intermediate
Finished Quilt: 42" x 47"
Finished Block: approx. 12" x 14" (7 star blocks)

Fabric Requirements
(Measurements are in yards unless otherwise indicated)

If the design repeat of Main Fabric A is		6"–10"	11"–14"	15"–20"	21"–27"	over 27"
You will need this many yards	Wall*	2	3¾	4	5¼	6 repeats
	Queen	5¼	5¼	5¼	5¼	6 repeats

Additional Fabrics	Wall	Queen
Background Fabric B	1½	4½
Border Fabric C	¼ border 1	3⅞
Accent Fabric D		1½
Backing (piece crosswise)	2 ¾	9
Binding (cut 2½" strips crosswise)	½	1

* Includes border 2.

Whacking 60° Diamonds

I found that these blocks went together more easily when the straight grain ran down the center of the diamond. While other whacking methods begin with a crosswise strip, you will need to whack the stack a little differently for these projects to get the grain line positioned correctly. You may want to practice first on a single layer of scrap fabric. Check a piece with the accuracy guide on page 109 to make sure you are getting the correct angle.

Whacking Main Fabric Diamonds for the Block Kits

The illustrations show the stack for the Morning Star queen quilt. If you are doing the wall quilt, the guide piece will be shorter, but the same directions apply.

1. Refer to the Stack-n-Whack chart for your project to determine the size of the guide piece. Using the basic stacking method, cut and stack six identical layers of Main Fabric A.

2. Trim about ¼" from the pinned edge of the fabric stack, if necessary, to get a smooth, straight edge. Depending on the brand of ruler, you can use the 30° line or the 60° line for the first cut. Place the ruler on the fabric with the angle line along the raw edge (Figure 7-1) or along the selvage (Figure 7-2). Make sure that the angle of the ruler looks like the illustration. Cut the angle as shown, creating a large triangle. If necessary, cut part way, then carefully slide the ruler along the cut edge to finish cutting.

3. Place the large triangle as shown (Figure 7-3) and lay the long edge of the ruler down with the 3½" line on the bias edge. Cut a strip.

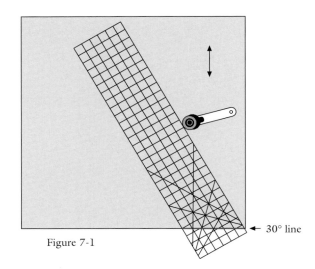

Figure 7-1 ← 30° line

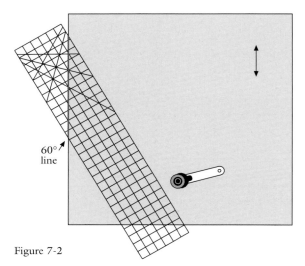

60° line

Figure 7-2

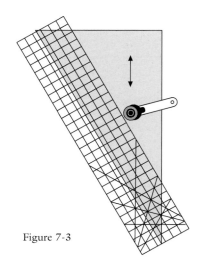

Figure 7-3

4. Carefully turn the strip set so that it lies as shown in Figure 7-4. You will see that one end of the strip has the "correct" angle. Do not use that end. If you do, your grain line will not go down the center of the diamond. Instead, place the ruler at the opposite end of the strip and trim that end with the same angle line you used in Step 2. The odd-shaped piece you trim off is scrap fabric.

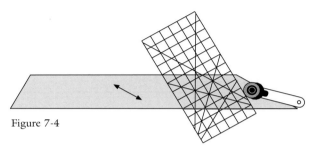

Figure 7-4

5. Turn the strip set around 180° (one half turn). Measure 3½" over from the angled edge and line up the 30° or 60° angle line along one straight edge for greater accuracy (Figure 7-5). Make your cut. This set of six identical diamonds is one block kit. Pin the kit together and set it aside. Continue cutting block kits from this strip (Figure 7-6). Each stack of diamonds is a block kit. Note the grain line. Using the accuracy guide in the Guides and Patterns, page 109, make sure the diamonds are the correct size.

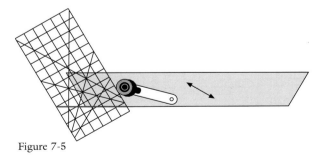

Figure 7-5

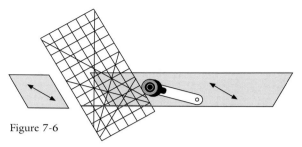

Figure 7-6

6. Cut additional strips and block kits from the large triangle in the same way. When you cut the strips from the remaining stacked section (Figure 7-7), you may need to cut part way, then slide the ruler to finish cutting the strip. Cut the number of block kits required for your project.

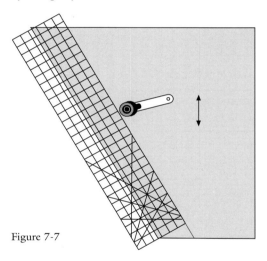

Figure 7-7

Whacking Accent Diamonds

Cut the accent diamonds used in the border of the Morning Star queen quilt in the same manner as the main fabric: Cut and stack four 21" x 22" non-identical rectangles of Fabric D and follow Steps 2 through 6 to cut 68 diamonds (17 stacks of 4).

Cutting Main Fabric A

Follow the directions for whacking 60° Diamonds on page 86.

Stack-n-Whack Chart for Morning Star Wall Quilt

Guide Piece...	Stack...	Whack...	To Make...
21" wide x one full repeat long	6 identical repeats of Main Fabric A	enough 3½" strips	(7) 60° diamond block kits
For fabrics with a repeat under 11", you will need a second stack.			

Stack-n-Whack Chart for Morning Star Queen Quilt

Guide Piece...	Stack...	Whack...	To Make...
21" wide x one full repeat long*	6 identical repeats of Main Fabric A	enough 3½" strips	(39) 60° diamond block kits
You will need two stacks of six repeats. Cut at least 20 block kits from each stack.			
*For fabrics with a repeat under 10", use three full repeats for the length of the guide piece. For fabrics with a repeat of 10" to 22", use two full repeats for the length of the guide piece.			

For cutting Fabric B and C 60° triangles, refer to the directions on pages 74-75.

Cutting Background Fabric B – Wall Quilt

Position	First Cut	Second Cut	Third Cut
Small Block Triangles	(5) 3¾" strips across width	(84) 60° triangles (17 per strip)	
Large Border Triangles	(2) 6¾" strips across width	(12) 60° triangles (9 per strip)	
Border Half-Triangles	(1) 7½" strips across width	(6) 60° triangles	Cut up the center on the straight grain to make 12 half-triangles
Top and Bottom Background Borders	(2) 2¼" strips across width		

Cutting Background Fabric B – Queen Quilt

Fabric and Position	First Cut	Second Cut
Small – Block and Border Triangles	(30) 3¾" strips across width	(524) 60° triangles (18 per strip)
Large Border Triangles	(6) 6¾" strips across width	(50) 60° triangles (9 per strip)

Cutting Fabrics C and D – Queen Quilt

Fabric and Position	First Cut	Second Cut	Third Cut
Fabric C Small Border Triangles	(5) 3¾" strips across width	(80) 60° triangles (17 per strip)	
Fabric C Large Border Triangles	(13) 6¾" strips across width	(112) 60° triangles (9 per strip)	
Fabric C Border Half-Triangles	(3) 7½" strips across width	(16) 60° triangles (7 per strip)	Cut up the center on the straight grain to make (32) half-triangles
Fabric D Border Diamonds	(4) rectangles 21" x 22" (stack)	(68) 3½" 60° diamonds	

Piecing the Morning Star Blocks

You can use the diamonds in each block kit with either tip in the center. You may want to lay out the pieces and preview the block each way before sewing, as the results can be dramatically different (Figure 7-8A and B). Once you have decided which end you would like in the center, place a reference pin at that end on each diamond in the block kit (Figure 7-9). The pin will remind you not to sew triangles to the sides adjacent to the center point.

1. Place the block kit (six identical diamonds) next to your machine with the end of the diamond that will be the center (the end with the reference pin) closest to you.

Figures 7-8A–B

Figure 7-9

Sew a background triangle to the top right edge of the diamond, placing the straight-grain edge of the triangle as shown by the arrow (Figure 7-10A). The top corner of the triangle should line up with the diamond tip; the triangle will extend ¼" at the lower end. Finger press the triangle open (Figure 7-10B). Repeat for the other five diamonds. You can remove the reference pins at this time.

Figures 7-10A–B

2. Turn the diamonds so that the center tips face you and add background triangles to the opposite sides, again lining up the tip of the triangle with the tip of the diamond (Figure 7-11A). Carefully press the finished triangle units from the right side, pressing the allowances toward the background (Figure 7-11B).

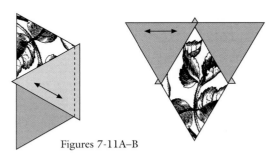

Figures 7-11A–B

3. Sew two triangle units together, matching the triangle tips and the seams of the diamonds (Figure 7-12A). Clip the triangle tips. Repeat with a second pair of triangle units (Figure 7-12B). Press allowances open.

4. Add a third triangle unit to each pair (Figure 7-13), matching the center seam. Clip the triangle tips. Press allowances open.

5. You now have two identical half-blocks (Figure 7-14). Do not sew them together, yet. This step comes when the blocks are assembled. Use a pin to keep the halves together until you are ready to lay out the quilt.

Figures 7-12A–B

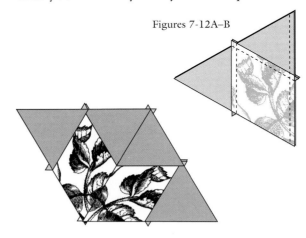

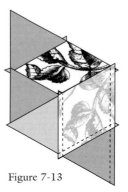

Figure 7-13

Figure 7-14: Do not sew the half-hexagon sections together yet.

Piece 7 Morning Star blocks/*39 for the queen*, following the illustrated instructions on page 89. Be sure to leave the half-blocks separate for now. If you have not yet chosen the border and accent fabrics, lay some of the star block halves on various fabrics and select them.

Piecing the Background Half-Blocks

Piece together four half-blocks to fill in the background on the top and bottom rows (see Wall Quilt Assembly diagram on page 93). For each half-block, use three 6¾" triangles of Background Fabric B.

Assembling the Wall Quilt

1. Working from the center of the quilt out, arrange the blocks according to the quilt assembly diagram on page 93. Fill in the top and bottom rows with the background half-blocks. Refer to page 78 to see how to add the half-triangles to the left and right sides of each row.

2. When you are satisfied with your layout, pin and sew the first row of half-blocks together. Clip the triangle tips that extend beyond the seam allowances after you sew each seam. Press allowances open. Return the row to your layout. Repeat for the remaining rows.

3. Sew the rows together, taking care to match the tips of the diamonds. Clip the tips that extend beyond the seam allowances and press the allowances open or to one side.

4. Measure the width across the center of the quilt and cut the 2¼" strips of Background Fabric B to this length. Pin and sew these strips to the top and bottom edges.

Adding the Borders – Wall Quilt	
Fabric and Position	**Cut**
Accent Fabric C – Border 1	(4) 1½" strips across width
Main Fabric A – Border 2	(4) 3½" strips x 42", cut lengthwise or across width

1. For the butted borders, measure the length down the center of the quilt and trim two strips of Accent Fabric C to this length. Pin and sew these borders to the quilt.

2. Measure the width across the center of the quilt, including side borders, and trim the other two strips of Accent Fabric C to this length. Pin and sew these borders.

3. Add the border of Main Fabric A in the same manner.

Plate 53: CHRISTMAS MORNING STAR by author, 1997. This arrangement is sometimes called SEVEN SISTERS. (Morning Star wall quilt directions begin on page 85.)

Piecing the Border Units – Queen Quilt

Piece together the units shown in the border unit diagram on page 94 (Fabrics B, C and D).

Assembling the Queen Quilt

You will need a flat area, such as a design wall (page 15), on which to preview the whole quilt top as you lay it out.

1. Working from the center of the quilt out, arrange the Morning Star blocks and border units according to quilt assembly diagram on page 94.

2. When you are satisfied with your layout, pin and sew the first vertical row of half-blocks together from top to bottom. Clip the triangle tips after you sew each seam. Press allowances toward the bottom of the quilt. Return the row to your layout.

3. Repeat the process with each vertical row, taking care to match the tips of the diamonds. Press allowances in every other row up, alternate rows down, to reduce the bulk when the rows are sewn together.

4. Sew the rows together, matching the seams and completing the star blocks. Clip the triangle tips and press the allowances to one side.

Finishing the Quilt

See Chapter Eight for suggestions on quilting design and binding. Prepare the backing by piecing together two 1⅜-yard lengths of backing fabric/*three 3-yard lengths for queen*. Layer, quilt, and bind.

Morning Star
Wall Quilt Assembly

Color Key	
☐	Main Fabric A
▨	Background Fabric B

Morning Star Queen Quilt Border Units

(6)Unit B   (18)Unit C1   (16)Unit C2   (16)Unit C3   To add the half-triangles for Units C2 and C3, see page 78.

(28)Unit Triangle 1   (28)Unit Triangle 2   (12)Unit Triangle 3   Use these Triangle Units to make the Half-Hexagons below.

(2)Unit D1   (2)Unit D2   (2)Unit E1   (2)Unit E2

(8)Unit F1   (6)Unit F2   (10)Unit G1   (10)Unit G2

Color Key
- ☐ Main Fabric A
- ▨ Background Fabric B
- ☐ Border Fabric C
- ▨ Accent Fabric D

Morning Star Queen Quilt Assembly

Chapter Eight
The Curtain Call

Back Art

You have pulled the proverbial rabbit out of your hat and stolen the show. Take a bow and give yourself a hardy round of applause.

You may choose to add "back art" for creative or practical reasons. I pieced the back of my Morning Star quilt (Plate 54) because I did not want to buy another nine yards of fabric. I did have to buy more of the background print, and the piecing took a lot longer than two straight seams would have, but I felt the extra effort was worthwhile.

Admirers of your Magic Stack-n-Whack quilt are likely to ask how many different fabrics you used and may not believe you when you tell them all the blocks came from a single print. If you have some of the main print left over, it is fun to provide "proof" by piecing some of it into the back.

You can plan to center the back design or use a more casual approach as I did for the back of my Diamond Ring quilt (Plate 55). I started with a piece of the main print and continued to add strips of various widths from my stash until I had a piece big enough for the back.

Quilting Designs and Strategies

A carefully chosen, well-executed quilting design often makes the difference between a good quilt and an outstanding one. Quilting creates dimension and texture through the play of light and shadow on the surface. You can use quilting to your advantage, drawing a viewer's eye to the aspects of the quilt you want to highlight, while de-emphasizing areas that are less important.

A detailed description of quilting methods would fill another book, and there are many good references available on this topic (see the Bibliography, page 111). Rather than giving you general quilting information, I would like to provide you with some specific advice about quilting the projects in this book so that you can show your "magic" quilt to best advantage.

You can begin thinking about your quilting plan while you are piecing the top. Are the blocks strikingly different? Consider overall quilting. This will give the quilt a unified surface and let each block stand on its own merits. A symmetrical pattern, repeated in each block, is another simple approach for these quilts. If the blocks show more subtle variations, you may want to emphasize the differences between them by quilting each one individually. If your quilt has large areas of background, such as the Kaleidoscope Pinwheel, you may want to add a quilting motif to these areas.

As you quilt your project, remember one key point of quilting design: The areas that come forward and attract the viewer are the areas that you do not quilt. Quilting flattens the surface and makes the unquilted areas stand out. So, if you have an area you would like to feature, quilt around it. Over-quilting the kaleidoscope blocks will not make them stand out; it is likely to have the opposite effect.

On the other hand, too little quilting can also detract from the finished quilt. It is hard to

Plate 54: Back view of IT'S NOT THE LATI-TUDE, IT'S THE ATTITUDE by author, 1997. The "back art" frames the main print with fabrics and shapes from the quilt top.

Plate 55: Back view of 48 PARROT DIA-MOND RING by author, 1996. This back mixes the main fabric with a casual collection of related prints.

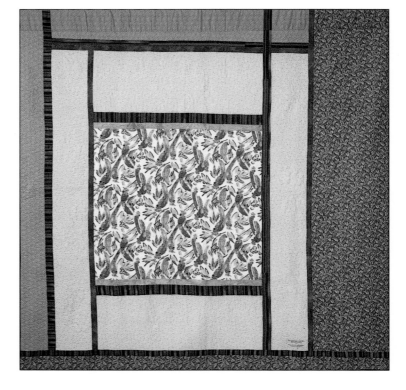

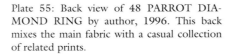

see the design when it has to compete with puffs and fabric wrinkles. Quilting down your background areas will help to highlight the blocks, making them "pop" from the surface. Quilting can also help hide the seams in the background areas.

Quilting the Magic Blocks

For the samples in this book, several strategies for quilting the kaleidoscope blocks have been used.

Concentric circles (Figure 8-1) will enhance most of the projects. You can see this approach in Botannica (detail, page 9) and Arabesque (page 68). You can also use a simple quilting motif, repeated in each section of the block (Figure 8-2). Hand quilting and machine-guided quilting can be used for these designs. If your experience with free-motion quilting is limited, be sure to practice on a sample quilt sandwich first.

Figure 8-2

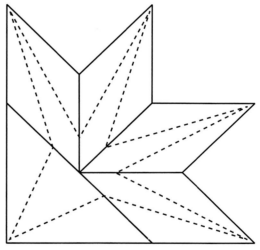
Figure 8-3: Full-size template on page 105.

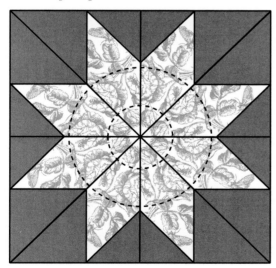
Figure 8-1

For the Hybrid Lilies quilt, straight lines were quilted within the lily flowers and bases to give them more dimension (Figure 8-3). You could substitute the curved petal design (Figure 8-4). This motif also fits the LeMoyne Star and Hands All Around blocks.

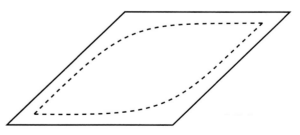
Figure 8-4: Full-size templates on pages 105 and 107.

To bring out the unique patterns in each block, you can quilt around the same part of the print in each segment of the block (Figure 8-5). Study each block before you quilt it to see what shapes you want to enhance.

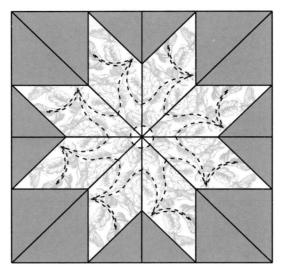

Figure 8-5

Quilting Motifs for Background Areas

The lobed leaf design (Figure 8-6A) fits in the background areas around the 15" Pinwheel blocks. The smooth leaf (Figure 8-6B) fits between the Pinwheel Plus blocks. I usually choose organic motifs like leaves for free-motion quilting; no one will argue if each comes out a little different, just as in nature. A little heart design (Figure 8-7) fits in the corners of the 9" LeMoyne Star blocks. You can point the hearts toward the center of each block, as I have done, or point them away from the center so that the heart tips come together in the background areas between the blocks.

Figures 8-6A–B: Full-size templates on page 104.

Figure 8-7. This motif is full-size.

For the Hybrid Lily quilt, you may choose to repeat the lily motif in the center square with quilting or trapunto (Figure 8-8). To make a quilting pattern, trace the outline of one of the finished blocks. Go over the tracing with a permanent marker, using a straight edge to smooth out the lines.

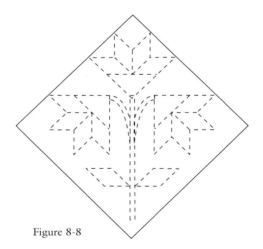

Figure 8-8

Transfer the design to the center square. For machine trapunto, place a layer of polyester batting under the quilt square and baste it in place on the outline. (Using water-soluble thread in either the needle or the bobbin.) Turn the piece over and trim the batting close to the stitching. Be careful not to clip the fabric. Leave the batting in place behind the lily design. Remove the water-soluble thread from the machine and replace it with your quilting thread. Layer the top and backing with your choice of batting, and quilt as usual, going over the basting lines. The basting lines will dissolve in water, leaving just the final row of stitching. (For more on machine trapunto, see Hari Walner's book listed in the Bibliography, page 111.)

Overall Quilting

The scale of the quilting pattern is important. Closely spaced quilting will enhance the graphics of the top. A pattern that is too large will overwhelm the blocks and draw attention only to itself.

If you are a machine quilter, you will appreciate the convenience of continuous-line designs. I have included some of these designs in this chapter.

The continuous-curve designs (Figure 8-9) fit the Hexagon Star projects. You will find that machine-guided quilting makes this design easy to do. Begin at one corner and follow the curve to the second corner. Continue from one triangle to the next, alternating left and right curves, so you create a serpentine line across the quilt. When you reach an outside corner, turn the quilt and come back across it on another set of lines. Eventually, you will have quilted on all three sides of each triangle, with a minimum number of starts and stops. (This is one of those things that will make more sense when you do it.)

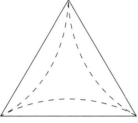

Figure 8-9: Full-size templates on pages 108 and 109.

The zigzag (Figure 8-10) and serpentine (Figure 8-11) patterns are favorites of mine

because they are designed for free-motion quilting. With the zigzag pattern, stop with the needle down each time you change direction to get points. For the serpentine effect, make gentle curves at each turn. You can adapt either pattern for any of the diamond or 60° triangle projects. Stitch from one triangle or diamond to the next, taking slow, careful stitches through the intersections of the piecing. For diamond shapes, this pattern fills the piece in one pass and requires little or no marking. For It's Not the Latitude, It's the Attitude (Plate 52, page 84), I quilted the entire top with this pattern. I did have to mark some guide lines in the border triangles, because the diamond piecing did not extend through the border. For 60° triangles, use the marking guide (Figures 8-12) and quilt from one segment of the triangle to one segment of the next triangle, as described previously for the continuous-curve design, until you have quilted all the segments in each triangle (Figure 8-13). Starfish And Sea Urchins (Plate 51, page 81) shows the continuous serpentine design used in the star points and blue border triangles.

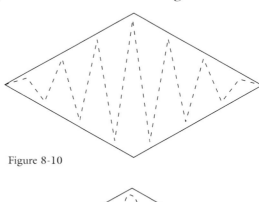

Figure 8-10

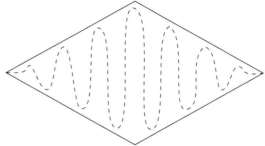

Figure 8-11

I often use a combination strategy, quilting the "magic" blocks individually or with concentric circles, and quilting the background and/or border areas with meander quilting or one of the continuous designs.

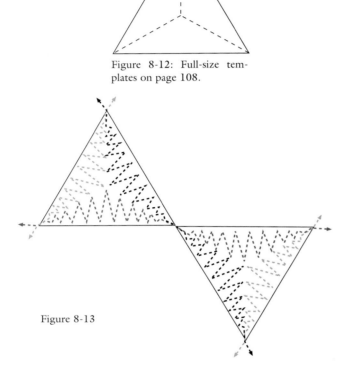

Figure 8-12: Full-size templates on page 108.

Figure 8-13

Finishing with a Flourish: Bindings, Sleeves, and Labels

Bindings

Bindings add strength to the edges of your quilts. Since none of these projects have curved edges, a double-fold, straight-grain binding will do nicely. Most quilters find this method easier to do than bias binding. You can use the same fabric as your outer border or provide a little accent with a contrasting binding.

Cut your binding strips on the lengthwise or crosswise grain of the fabric. For a ⅜" finished binding, cut 2½" strips. Piece together enough strips to make a binding long enough to go around the perimeter of the quilt, including about 12" for turning corners and finishing the ends.

Piecing the strips on the diagonal (Figure 8-14) will stagger the seam allowances for a smoother binding. Trim the excess fabric, leaving ¼" allowances, and press the allowances open.

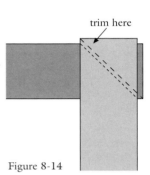

trim here

Figure 8-14

Press the binding strip in half lengthwise, wrong sides together. Press one end at a right angle and trim the corner to ¼" from the fold line (Figure 8-15).

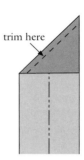

trim here

Figure 8-15

If you want to add a sleeve for hanging your quilt on a wall, read the section about sleeves, starting on page 101, before sewing on the binding.

Beginning part way down one side of your quilt, place the binding strip on the quilt top, right sides together and raw edges aligned. Leave about 3" unsewn at the beginning of the binding to allow for finishing (Figure 8-16). Sew the binding in place with a ⅜" seam allowance (on

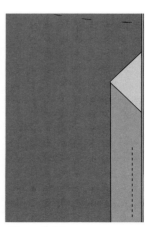

Figure 8-16

most machines, the width of the all-purpose presser foot will be about right). As you approach each corner, stop stitching ⅜" from the raw edge of the quilt top at the corner. With the needle down, turn the quilt a quarter-turn. Backstitch straight back to the raw edge of the quilt and raise the needle and the presser foot (Figure 8-17). Fold the binding up at a 45° angle and then down, matching the second fold to the raw edge of the quilt (Figures 8-18A–B). Begin stitching at the folded edge of the binding and continue to the next corner.

Figure 8-17

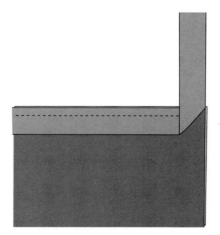

Figure 8-18A

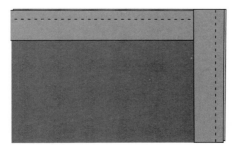

Figure 8-18B

When you come around to the first side again, stop stitching 3" or 4" from the beginning end. Lay the tail end along the raw edge, overlapping the beginning angled end and smooth in place. Cut the tail end so that it overlaps the beginning end by ¼" to ½" (Figure 8-19). Tuck the tail end into the beginning end. Finish stitching the binding in place (Figure 8-20).

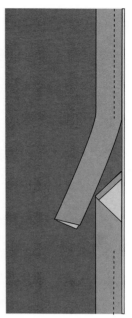

Figure 8-19

Figure 8-20   Bring the folded edge of the binding around to the back and blindstitch it in place, tucking in the corners to form neat miters (Figures 8-21A–B). Blindstitch the angled edge where the ends meet (Figure 8-22).

Sleeves

If you plan to hang your quilt or enter it in a show, consider adding a hanging sleeve as you sew the binding. This method saves time and results in a sleeve that will evenly distribute the weight of the quilt.

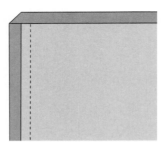

Figure 8-21A

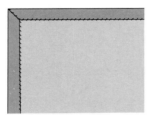

Figure 8-21B

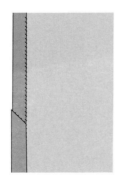

Figure 8-22

Prepare the sleeve by cutting a rectangle of fabric that is about 2" shorter than the width of the quilt. The sleeve width should be about 12" for bed quilts. For small wall quilts, 8" will suffice. Hem the short ends of the sleeve and press it in half lengthwise, wrong sides together.

Add the binding to the front of the quilt, but do not bring the folded edge around to the back yet. On the back of the quilt, center the sleeve along the top edge and pin it in place. Stitch it to the quilt with a scant ⅜" seam (just inside the seam allowances for the binding). Bring the binding around to the back and finish as directed previously, catching the sleeve and the quilt back as you finish the top edge.

Blindstitch the lower layer of the sleeve ends and the folded edge of the sleeve to the quilt back (Figure 8-23).

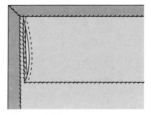

Figure 8-23

Take a Bow!

Label your quilt with your name, the date, and any other information you feel is important. This is good for your ego, and it will be a blessing for your descendants and future quilt historians.

Guides and Patterns

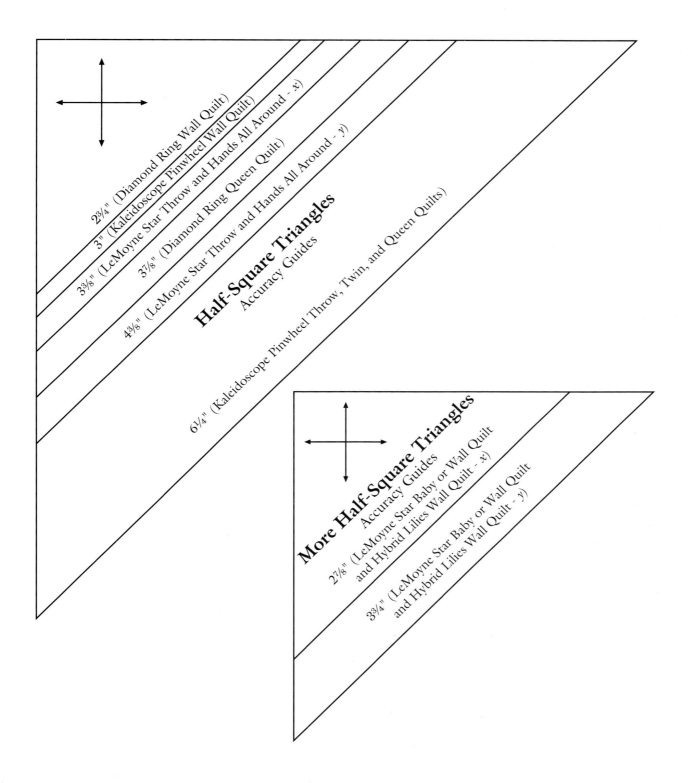

2¾" (Diamond Ring Wall Quilt)

3" (Kaleidoscope Pinwheel Wall Quilt)

3⅜" (LeMoyne Star Throw and Hands All Around - *x*)

3⅞" (Diamond Ring Queen Quilt)

4⅜" (LeMoyne Star Throw and Hands All Around - *y*)

Half-Square Triangles
Accuracy Guides

6¼" (Kaleidoscope Pinwheel Throw, Twin, and Queen Quilts)

More Half-Square Triangles
Accuracy Guides

2⅞" (LeMoyne Star Baby or Wall Quilt
and Hybrid Lilies Wall Quilt - *x*)

3¾" (LeMoyne Star Baby or Wall Quilt
and Hybrid Lilies Wall Quilt - *y*)

Pinwheel
Quilting Patterns

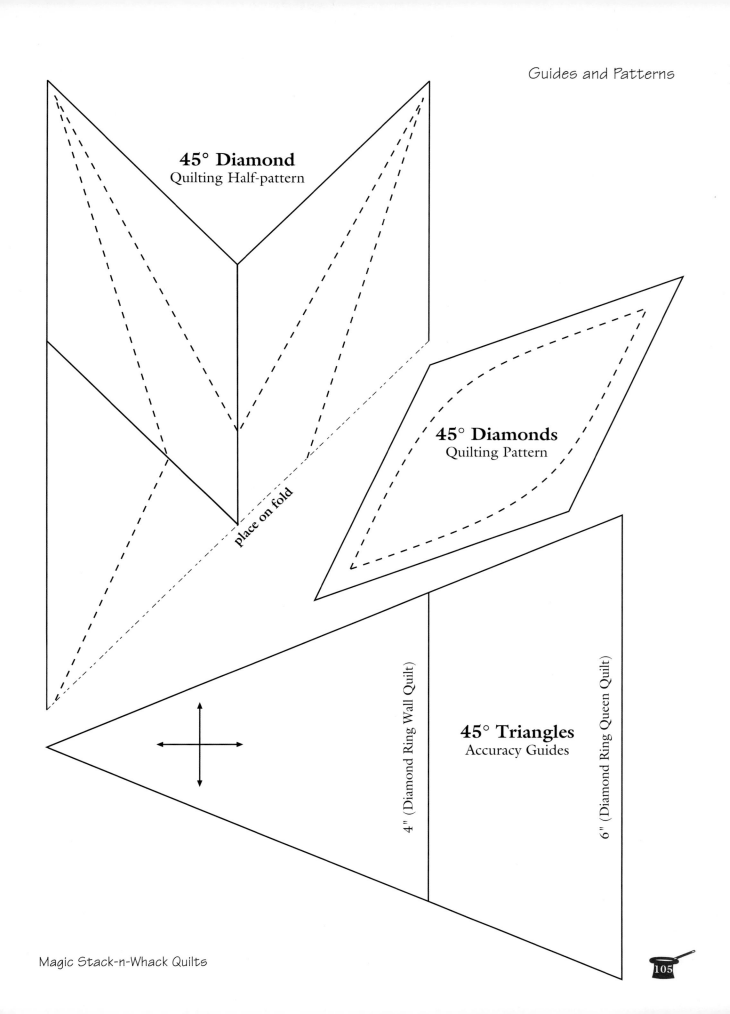

45° Diamond
Quilting Half-pattern

place on fold

45° Diamonds
Quilting Pattern

4" (Diamond Ring Wall Quilt)

45° Triangles
Accuracy Guides

6" (Diamond Ring Queen Quilt)

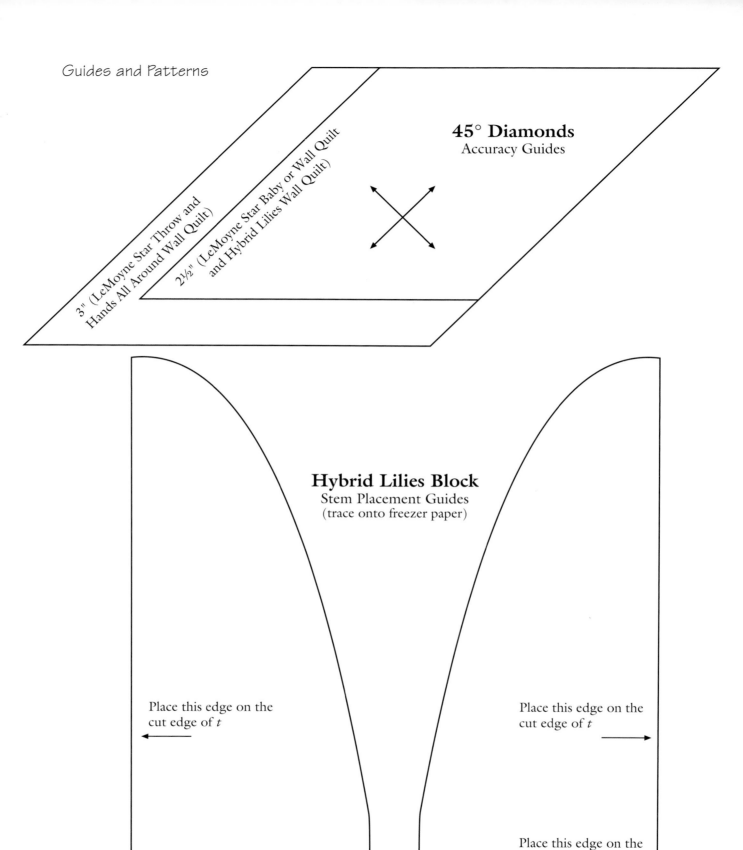

45° Diamonds
Accuracy Guides

3" (LeMoyne Star Throw and
Hands All Around Wall Quilt)

2½" (LeMoyne Star Baby or Wall Quilt
and Hybrid Lilies Wall Quilt)

Hybrid Lilies Block
Stem Placement Guides
(trace onto freezer paper)

Place this edge on the
cut edge of *t*

Place this edge on the
cut edge of *t*

Place this edge on the
cut edge of *s* and *t*

Place this edge on the
cut edge of *s* and *t*

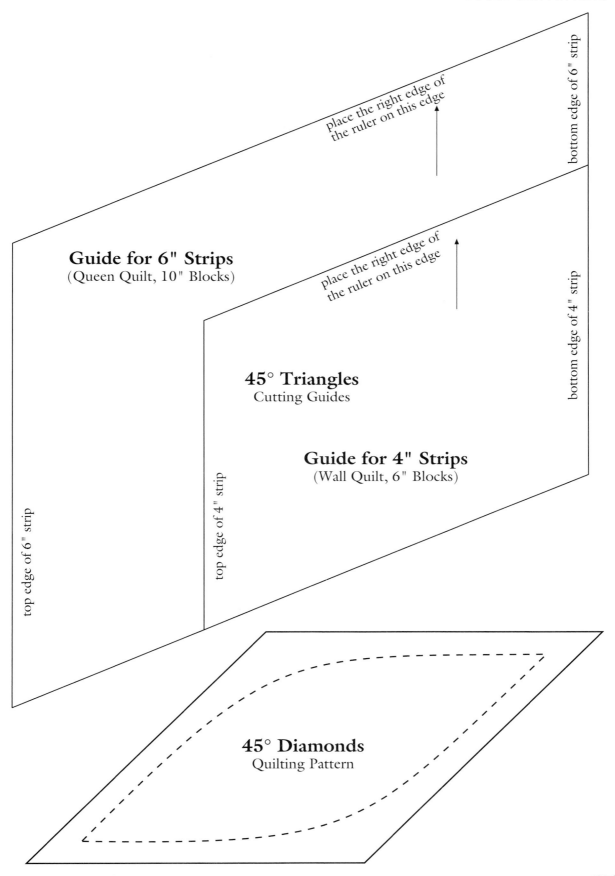

place the right edge of the ruler on this edge

bottom edge of 6" strip

Guide for 6" Strips
(Queen Quilt, 10" Blocks)

place the right edge of the ruler on this edge

bottom edge of 4" strip

45° Triangles
Cutting Guides

Guide for 4" Strips
(Wall Quilt, 6" Blocks)

top edge of 6" strip

top edge of 4" strip

45° Diamonds
Quilting Pattern

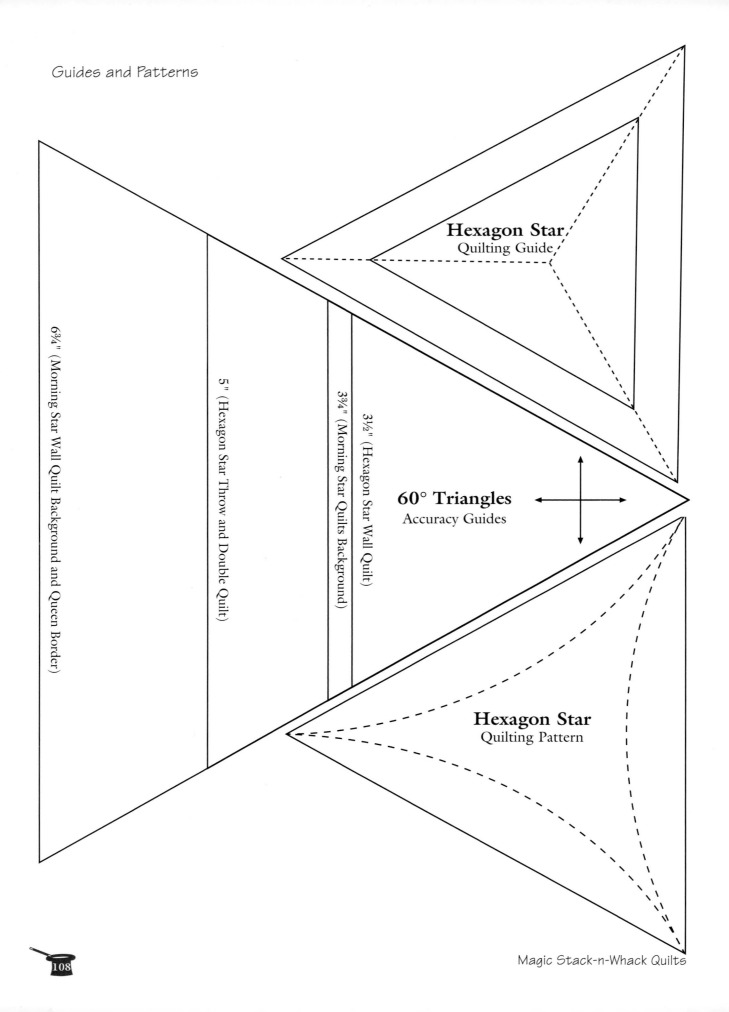

Hexagon Star
Quilting Guide

6¾" (Morning Star Wall Quilt Background and Queen Border)

5" (Hexagon Star Throw and Double Quilt)

3¾" (Morning Star Quilts Background)

3½" (Hexagon Star Wall Quilt)

60° Triangles
Accuracy Guides

Hexagon Star
Quilting Pattern

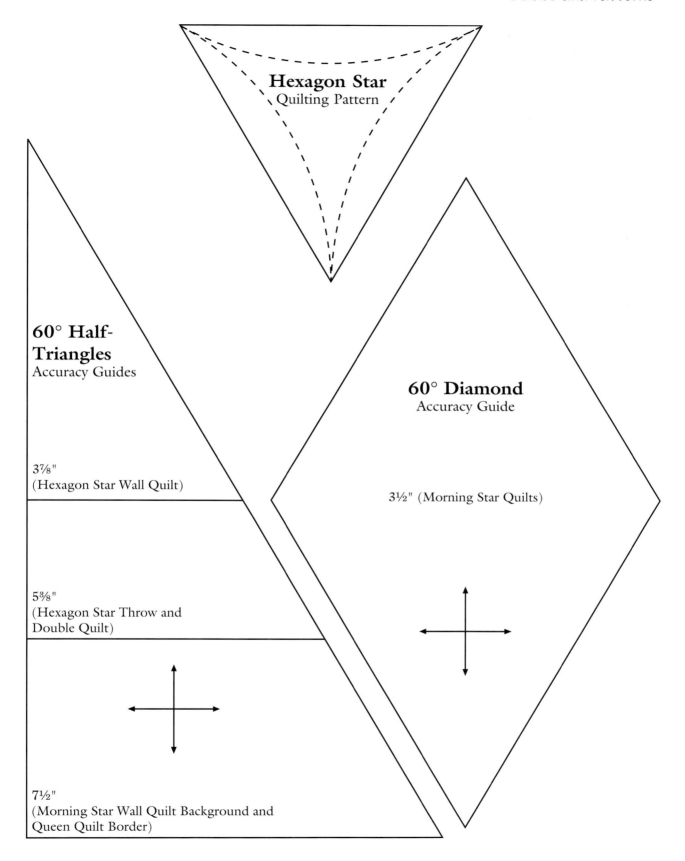

Hexagon Star
Quilting Pattern

**60° Half-
Triangles**
Accuracy Guides

3⅞"
(Hexagon Star Wall Quilt)

5⅜"
(Hexagon Star Throw and
Double Quilt)

7½"
(Morning Star Wall Quilt Background and
Queen Quilt Border)

60° Diamond
Accuracy Guide

3½" (Morning Star Quilts)

Lesson Plans

Magic Stack-n-Whack classes are tremendously fun because students see quick results and enjoy watching the blocks come together. Teachers and shop owners are welcome to develop classes using this book as a textbook. Please remember that the book's copyright prohibits photocopying or other printing of any materials herein for commercial use. Pages with quilting patterns, cutting guides, or placement guides (pages 98, 103–109) may be photocopied for personal use. The following suggestions for lesson plans were designed to fit various class schedules.

One-Day Workshop

Using Stack-n-Whack rotary-cutting methods, students cut a large-print fabric of their choice and piece several blocks with magical kaleidoscope effects.

Recommended Projects: Wall or throw sizes of the Kaleidoscope Pinwheel, Pinwheel Plus, LeMoyne Star, Hexagon Star, and Morning Star quilts.

Two Three-Hour Classes

In two half-day or evening sessions, students learn the Magic Stack-n-Whack rotary cutting method and piece the blocks for their quilts. Students often can't wait until the second class to finish their blocks. If they have already finished them, they can set their blocks together in the second class.

Session 1. Cut the main fabric and the background fabric, and begin piecing the blocks. Allow time to preview accent fabrics.

Session 2: Finish piecing the blocks. Review setting and finishing steps.

Recommended Projects: Any of the Half-Square Triangle, 45° Diamond, or 60° Triangle projects and the Morning Star Wall Quilt.

Four Two-Hour Classes

In four two-hour sessions, students learn the Magic Stack-n-Whack cutting method and piece a one-of-a-kind quilt. This longer format allows more time for help with fabric selection and layout decisions.

Session 1. Cut the main fabric for the blocks and preview the block kits on various backgrounds. Students can then cut the background fabric at home.

Session 2. Begin sewing the blocks. If the design calls for an accent fabric, allow some time to preview possibilities during class.

Session 3. Complete the blocks and decide on the arrangement. Pin the blocks to a sheet to keep them in order. Begin preparing the setting and border pieces.

Session 4. Sew quilt together. Discuss quilting and finishing options.

Recommended Projects: Any of the designs in the book. Larger projects, such as the Diamond Ring, Hexagon Star, and Morning Star bed quilts, will need more wall space during the layout session and may require more sewing at home between classes.

Bibliography

Cleland, Lee. *Quilting Makes the Quilt*. That Patchwork Place, Bothell, WA, 1995.

Marston, Gwen and Joe Cunningham. *Quilting with Style*. American Quilter's Society, Paducah, KY, 1993.

Noble, Maurine. *Machine Quilting Made Easy*. That Patchwork Place, Bothell, WA, 1994.

Walner, Hari. *Trapunto by Machine*. C&T Publishing, Lafayette, CA, 1996.

Sources

Hancock's
(Flower-head pins, rotary-cutting supplies, wide selection of fabric)
3841 Hinkleville Road
Paducah, KY 42001
800-845-8723 or (502) 443-4410
website: http://hancocks-paducah.com

Nancy's Notions
333 Beichl Avenue, PO Box 683
Beaver Dam, WI 53916-0683
800-245-5116
(Flower-head pins, seam rolls, pressing mats with grids)

Mary Stori
6 Coldren Drive
Prospect Heights, IL 60070
(To order a kit for a Portable Free-Standing Flannel Wall, including instructions, diagrams, and 12 plastic clips, send a check for $20 (shipping included). The kit includes a materials list for the required purchase of PVC pipe, fittings, and flannel. Directions are for an 84" wide x 76" high wall, but you may easily customize the size to fit your needs.)

OTHER AQS BOOKS

This is only a small selection of the books available from the American Quilter's Society. AQS books are known worldwide for timely topics, clear writing, beautiful color photos, and accurate illustrations and patterns. The following books are available from your local bookseller, quilt shop, or public library.

#5850	US$22.95
#5589	US$21.95
#5176	US$24.95
#5755	US$21.95
#5296	US$16.95
#5339	US$19.95
#5708	US$22.95
#5852	US$19.95
#4831	US$22.95

Look for these books nationally or call **1-800-626-5420**